MONTH-BY-MONTH
ORGANIC GARDENING

A comprehensive guide to growing your own fruit and vegetables successfully, using nature's own resources to enrich the soil and combat pests and diseases.

MONTH-BY-MONTH ORGANIC GARDENING

The Green Gardener's Calendar

LAWRENCE D. HILLS
Founder and President of the Henry
Doubleday Research Association

Thorsons
An Imprint of HarperCollins*Publishers*

Thorsons
An Imprint of HarperCollins*Publishers*
77–85 Fulham Palace Road,
Hammersmith, London W6 8JB
1160 Battery Street,
San Francisco, California 94111–1213

Published by Thorsons 1983
Revised and updated edition published 1989
5 7 9 10 8 6 4

Line Illustrations by Nils Solberg

Colour photography courtesy of The Henry Doubleday
Research Association, Ryton-on-Dunsmore, Coventry

A catalogue record for this book
is available from the British Library

ISBN   0 7225 1863 3

Printed in Great Britain by Woolnough Bookbinding Limited,
Irthlingborough, Northamptonshire

CONTENTS

FOREWORD

In an age when so much money and effort is expended on the advertising and selling of chemical fertilizers and of newer pesticides, the survival and growth of the Organic Movement is a remarkable phenomenon.

Lawrence Hills has played a unique role in that survival and growth. He has the rare gift, as an expert, of being able – in simple language and striking metaphor – to make his expertise intelligible to the non-expert.

In his lectures, travels, writings and by the founding of the Henry Doubleday Research Association he has carried the torch of organic gardening throughout Britain and to other lands. The HDRA has three groups in Australia, one in New Zealand, another in India, and a sixth recently established in Sri Lanka.

For struggling organic gardeners like me, his books are a godsend; they comprise a veritable mine of valuable information and above all of practical advice.

This new book is written for those who seek more knowledge of the nutritive value of garden crops and who wish to grow their own fruit and vegetables for the health of their families.

There is sound evidence suggesting that much ill health in Britain, including certain birth defects, is due to mineral and vitamin deficiencies. Year by year new evidence accumulates of the vitally important part played by green leaf and fresh food vitamins such as folic acid and ascorbic acid in maintaining normal bodily functions. It is probably true that we have grossly underestimated the daily requirement of these and other vitamins.

We eat far too much refined sugar and white flour. These worthless, deprived foods displace natural foods – fruit, vegetables and wholegrain cereals – and so we suffer all the dire effects of vitamin, mineral and fibre deficiency, and from what T. L. Cleave termed 'over-consumption'.

As a nation we are constipated, our hospital waiting lists are loaded with hundreds of patients suffering from the complications of that distressing condition. Our national health will not improve until we discard worthless 'industrialized foods' and return to nature's own food, prepared with the minimum of human manipulation.

Readers of *Month-by-month Organic Gardening* will find a clear exposition of the botanical grouping of fruits and vegetables and details of their mineral and vitamin content. A masterful review of various methods of compost making is followed by a month-by-month account of the organic garden. We are carried along by the author's enthusiasm which has the effect of making us eager to rush out and 'get on with it'.

This book will inspire established organic gardeners to improve their methods and encourage newcomers to begin. It will do more for the health of the nation than much medicine.

Walter W. Yellowlees
MC, MB, Ch.B., FRCGP

PREFACE

I have written this book to help those who have health problems to garden their way out of them, for the healthiest of all health foods are those grown without chemicals in your own garden. In particular I am thinking of those with allergies or on special diets of all kinds, for whom the right food is better than any medicine. Therefore this book includes many tables of vitamins, minerals, and other substances of nutritional value, taken mainly from *The Composition of Foods* by R. A. McCance and E. M. Widdowson (HMSO, 1960) and *Bridges Food and Beverage Analysis* by Marjorie R. Mattice (Henry Kimpton, 1950). The figures relating to the least usual vegetables and many others are by Dr A. H. Ward, Analyst to the Henry Doubleday Research Associa-

tion. Other sources are acknowledged in the text.

Firstly, I would like to thank Dr William Yellowlees, President of the McCarrison Society, for his Foreword. I would also thank the Editor of *Garden News* for permission to use material that has appeared in my fortnightly organic gardening column. I would express my appreciation of the work of Nils Solberg for the line drawings that illustrate this book.

Finally, I must thank my wife, Hilda Cherry Hills, who knows far more about food than I do, for her help, her suggestions and her corrections. Books, like gardens, are always better when they are family affairs.

Lawrence D. Hills, D.Sc.

Shortly before his death in 1990, Lawrence D. Hills was granted an Honorary Doctorate by Coventry Polytechnic, in recognition of his outstanding international contribution to horticulture and environmental issues.

CHAPTER 1
THE ORGANIC GARDENER'S YEAR

The gardener's year starts slowly with seed catalogues and planning in January, but all too soon the tide of spring comes racing in over the shallow weeks, sweeping up to midsummer and ebbing slowly away to autumn and winter. Our crops have 'gardening diaries' inside them, kept by the changing length of the days, and when cold, dry springs hold them back, while the day length drives them on, they race ahead when the warm rain comes at last, until you can almost hear the whisper of their growth below the shouting of the weeds.

We feed the soil with organic manures and fertilizers, which wait for the sun to warm the living soil to life, so our crops start more slowly than those of our inorganic neighbours, whose chemicals are quicker, but ours catch up and finish with finer flavours and qualities that all organic gardeners know. Time matters more to us because we follow our crops rather than drive them.

This book is written to help organic gardeners keep up with the tides of the racing year, for so much of the art of using time to make space go further, and controlling pests and diseases by cunning rather than chemicals, depends on making the right choice among the jobs that clamour to be done before the light fades and another weekend is gone. It is more important to sow, plant or thin with the tide of life, than to mow and edge and tidy. It is less important to do the job very well, or neatly, than to do it at the right time when you are a beginner. With experience comes the ability to work both fast and well, as you learn the speed without haste that has fed the peasants of the world through the centuries.

Crop rotation

Not only do we need to take our crops round the year to bring us food for all seasons. We must take them round the garden so that each one helps the crop that follows, leaving the maximum interval to rest the soil and allow the disease spores and pests to die out rather than build up trouble for the future. The usual garden rotation is one of four beds, with potatoes, root crops, cabbage tribe and pea tribe following each other, so that it is four years before each group of crops grows in the same place.

Bed 1
Potatoes:
- earlies, followed by leeks
- maincrop, followed by broad beans.

Bed 2
Legumes:
- broad beans
- peas
- runner beans
- French beans
- haricot beans.

All peas and beans followed by young plants of Brussels sprouts, sprouting broccoli, cabbage.

Bed 3
Brassicas:
- cabbage tribe, planted as young plants in this bed the year before

- outdoor tomatoes after the winter cabbages are cleared
- lettuces, radishes, turnips or swedes.

Bed 4
Roots:
- onions
- carrots
- beetroot
- kohlrabi
- salsify
- parsnips
- lettuces.

Pests and diseases that can be controlled or prevented by rotation almost always follow families, and there are many of these with so few pests or diseases that they need not be rotated but fitted in wherever there is room. Lettuces, which belong to the daisy family *(Compositae)*, are an example. These and others in the same useful class are marked with an asterisk in Table 1. Those whose gardens are too small to grow enough potatoes to be worth the trouble could replace these with a bed of lettuce and the other salad crops that do not need rotation, while in very small gardens, especially those filled with clubroot spores by previous owners, it is possible to forget about rotations and grow only crops that do not need this method. If you merely cut out the potatoes and make yours a three-bed rotation, you are bringing the onions and cabbages back to the same place too soon.

The pea tribe
Members of the pea tribe have nitrogen-fixing bacteria in their roots, and organic gardeners sow as many of these as possible, to grow their own fertilizer rather than buying it in bags. Adding an extra bed of white-seeded runners for drying as butter or haricot beans gives extra concentrated storable protein, of value to vegetarians and those who wish to grow as much as possible of their

food in their own gardens, as well as even more nitrogen. Gardens with poor soil can be built up by adding a bed under 'green manure crops', which are usually nitrogen-fixers. After sowing they grow with relatively little trouble and can be dug in to build up fertility.

You cannot safely grow *only* the pea tribe, for this can build up a number of harmful soil fungi, as every construction-minded gardener finds when he concretes in permanent metal-piping 'goal post' structure to string his runner beans along. The spores of plant diseases dry and blow on the wind, can be carried on shoes and, in the case of clubroot, arrive on the roots of bought-in plants or manure. Generally speaking it is safest to think of your 'no-star' crops as like lightning – they should never strike the same place twice.

Potato eelworm cysts (white, yellow, or brown pinheads on the roots of plants that are stunted and giving smaller and smaller crops each year) and microscopic clubroot spores last up to nine years in the soil. Onion downy-mildew spores live on in roots and dug-in foliage for at least four years, and with the rising popularity of autumn-sown onions and perennials like the Welsh onion, this disease is increasing, and so is onion white rot. The strongest argument against the old garden custom of making up a permanent onion bed with plenty of soot, bonemeal and sulphate of potash, is the stem eelworm, *Dithylenchus dipsaci*, which causes onion bloat, with plants swelling at the base, leaves swollen and distorted, and cracked and rotting bulbs. This non-cyst-forming eelworm can also attack phlox in the herbaceous border and migrate to strawberries and parsnips, causing the same bloated and distorted stems and rotting of the crop.

The answer to these and many other soil problems is crop rotation, ideally longer than the usual four years. If you have room for it, a six-bed system is excellent: add a bed resting under green manures, or extra pea-tribe crops, and bring the strawberry bed into the rotation. The alternative is to cut down on the cabbage tribe if you have increasing clubroot trouble, keeping to the winter and spring crops like sprouting broccoli, and grow only early potatoes and spring-sown onions to reduce the build-up, a process helped by plenty of good compost, for all diseases are worst in chemically fed gardens.

Make your own rotation

Few gardeners want to grow every vegetable there is, and the best way of saving space is to grow only what you eat and enjoy. Therefore every garden needs its own rotation, which can be altered to suit changing tastes and by discarding failures, a process of experiment and adventure that is one of the many joys of gardening. Composing your own rotation needs knowledge of the tribes, or natural orders, of our crops. Pests and diseases run in families, like many other qualities. The vegetables in this book belong to thirteen natural orders, fifteen if you count the *Labiatae*, to which most herbs belong, and the *Rosaceae*, the rose family, which includes apples, pears, raspberries and strawberries. Only the last named need rotation.

Natural orders

The system of Natural Orders was devised by Carl Von Linne of Sweden (1707-78) (who called himself 'Linnaeus' because he used Latin which was then the international language of science), and recorded in his great work that has made the study of the living world possible. In an age that is likely to think that Plato is a washing-up liquid, the Latin names may be awkward for many gardeners, so they have been numbered for ease of reference, as given

at the bottom of Table 1. The most important to remember in planning rotations are: No. 4 – the *Cruciferae*, the Brassicas or cabbage family; No.7 – the *Leguminosae* or pea tribe; No. 8 – the *Liliaceae*, the onions, and No. 11 – the *Solanaceae*, to which potatoes, tomatoes, sweet peppers and aubergines belong.

Though there are only thirty-eight vegetables on this list, they have many varieties and it is their earliness, lateness and the length of time a single sowing stays in production that makes our gardens feed us so long and so well. There are about 300 varieties of potato, which include early – to dig and scrape first in July or even June, and second early – like Duke of York, which can be scraped as an early and dug to keep far into the spring when it grows large and is tasty baked in its jacket in September, leaving a better choice of winter crops to follow it than the maincrops which produce the highest yields, lifted in October.

Because of the Regulations we share with our fellow members of the EEC it is no longer possible for gardeners to buy a large number of vegetable varieties, many of which have been favourites for generations for flavour, or other qualities of garden value, such as thin skins in tomatoes. In June 1978 when these Regulations came into force, 874 distinct varieties, many of which had been grown on their merits for several centuries, and an additional 600 regarded by the Authorities as 'synonyms' – too alike to be worth distinguishing – were lost. The HDRA (the abbreviation by which the Henry Doubleday Research Association is known in all countries and that will be used throughout this book) fought these Regulations and lost. They continue to issue a seed catalogue that includes as many of these varieties as they can legally sell, together with newer flavour kinds as these are discovered.

Table 1: VEGETABLES IN THEIR ORDERS

Artichokes* (Jerusalem)	*Compositae*	Miner's lettuce*	*Portulaceae*
Beans	*Leguminosae*	New Zealand spinach*	*Aizoaceae*
Beetroot*	*Chenopodiaceae*	Onions	*Liliaceae*
Broccoli	*Cruciferae*	Parsley	*Umbelliferae*
Brussels sprouts	*Cruciferae*	Parsnips	*Umbelliferae*
Cabbages	*Cruciferae*	Peas	*Leguminosae*
Carrots	*Umbelliferae*	Potatatoes	*Solanaceae*
Cauliflowers	*Cruciferae*	Pumpkins*	*Cucurbitaceae*
Celeriac	*Umbelliferae*	Radishes	*Cruciferae*
Celery	*Umbelliferae*	Rhubarb*	*Polygonaceae*
Cucumbers*	*Cucurbitaceae*	Salsify*	*Compositae*
Hamburg parsley	*Umbelliferae*	Savoy cabbage	*Cruciferae*
Kale	*Cruciferae*	Scorzonera*	*Compositae*
Kohlrabi	*Cruciferae*	Shallots	*Liliaceae*
Lamb's lettuce*	*Valerianaceae*	Spinach	*Chenopodiaceae*
Landcress*	*Cruciferae*	Swedes	*Cruciferae*
Leeks	*Liliaceae*	Sweetcorn	*Gramineae*
Lettuces*	*Compositae*	Tomatoes	*Solanaceae*
Marrows*	*Cucurbitaceae*	Turnips	*Cruciferae*

NATURAL ORDERS BY NUMBER

Aizoaceae	1	*Liliaceae*	8
Chenopodiaceae	2	*Polygonaceae*	9
Compositae	3	*Portulacaceae*	10
Cruciferae	4	*Solanaceae*	11
Cucurbitaceae	5	*Umbelliferae*	12
Gramineae	6	*Valerianaceae*	13
Leguminosae	7		

Under the regulations, vegetable and farm seed varieties can now be patented, earning large sums in royalties, which has led to the takeover of most seed firms by multinational companies that are mainly concerned with the needs of commercial growers. The gardener should therefore choose new varieties for disease resistance, bearing in mind that even slight resistance is increased when vegetables are grown organically, and for good freezing qualities. Especially in cold gardens with short grow-ing seasons, as in Scotland, it pays to forget about succession and grow for a single crop that can be picked for a big freezing session.

Both these aspects are of great commercial value so seedsmen work to increase them. Flavour and garden qualities such as the ability to last without bolting for up to a month from a single sowing possessed by the lettuce Sutton's Windermere, are neglected so gardeners who find something outstanding should write and congratulate the firm that sells it, expressing the hope that they will keep it in cultivation. The motto of Industry today is far too often 'The *small* customer is always wrong' and gardeners who buy by the packet rather than the sackful receive the least consideration.

Bush and tree fruit are raised and sold by relatively small firms because, although their varieties can be patented, there are no large profits to be made like those that attract the world's biggest seedsmen, such as Royal Dutch Shell and Unilever. The situation, therefore, is entirely different with a wide choice available for those who wish to grow what they like in their own gardens. It is even possible by arrangement with specialist firms to have any one of the 1,888 varieties of apple in the National Fruit Trials collection at Brogdale Farm, Faversham, Kent, grafted to order. You can even obtain Flower of Kent, the variety, it is believed, that fell on Sir Isaac Newton's head and taught him the law of gravity!

The HDRA has compiled *The Good Fruit Guide*, describing over 1,000 bush and tree fruit varieties, what pollinates what, where to buy them and lists of those with frost-resistant blossom, for walls of every aspect and the nearest substitutes for Cox in northern gardens.

This can, of course, do nothing about the monstrous regiment of Golden Delicious which are not so much apples as 'permitted sweeteners'. The Golden Delicious variety is bred to take the maximum quantity of chemical nitrogen fertilizer for the largest and most highly sweetened crop. It is possible that the fall in cigarette smoking will lead to a greater appreciation of taste among young people, even in an age when the only way to enjoy flavour and health will be to grow fruit and vegetables in your own garden.

CHAPTER 2
DIGGING FOR A DIET

Everyone today is on a diet. Even the healthiest of us, happily eating just ordinary food, are 'dieted' by the food processors who have decided what it pays to make us eat by advertising, while inorganic farmers who use hormones and growth promotors can put additives even into simple steaks. The writing is on the packets and tins, but very small and no doubt legal until something happens and it has to be withdrawn. The only way to be sure of eating only what you choose to eat, is to buy it organically grown, or to grow it yourself, which is a great deal cheaper. Ask not at whom the fish finger points – it points at you!

It would be possible, but monotonous, to grow all your own food in your own garden, ideally supplemented by chickens and a goat. In practice we need to import our wheat for wholemeal bread, which is an ideal concentrated food with minerals and vitamins to digest it and make it the staff of a healthy life, but because we have taught birds to associate houses with food, it is not possible to grow wheat for home breadmaking in a small garden. As soon as it is ripe the birds will slaughter it, so buy your wheat from an organic farmer and grind it yourself to enjoy the full flavour of bread made from fresh milled flour. Or buy freshly ground flour from a food shop, for there is no reason why everyone should not enjoy home-baked bread. If you cannot tell the difference between real wholemeal and 'brown' give up smoking, for it is ruining your taste buds.

Organic and inorganic – the flavour difference

An even greater difference in flavour lies between organically grown and chemical-fed potatoes, and though these take up space in the garden, if possible grow all your own, even if you have to dig up your back lawn to do it. The potato is the gardener's best bargain in terms of food for space – about twice as much as the same area under wheat. Because it has the minerals and vitamins to digest its starches, these are not fattening, and it has a useful proportion of protein. Slimmers cut potatoes from their diet, because they would rather give up the tasteless and unattractive mush that is a poor-flavoured, high yielder like Pentland Crown, chemically fed, and eat biscuits instead. But a ½ pound (225 g) packet of starch-reduced slimming biscuits holds about as many carbohydrates as 3 pounds (1.4 kg) of potatoes, and without any vitamins to break them down. The pre-Potato Famine Irish were not fat, neither were the pre-Inca Peruvians, who also used potatoes as their staff of life.

The vitamins and minerals in vegetables

Because this book is concerned with gardening rather than nutrition these details are kept to a minimum. Table 2, however, shows why potatoes are always pushed in days of wartime rationing and why they are our most valuable vegetable.

The potato has the highest dry matter, carbohydrate and protein of any root

Table 2: COMPARATIVE VALUES OF POTATO AND OTHER FOODS

	Moisture (per cent)	Carbohydrate (per cent)	Protein (per cent)
Biscuits (average)	10.00	66.10	Variable, but low
White bread	33.80	55.50	Variable, but small
Potatoes (boiled)	76.40	19.70	2.10
Artichokes (boiled)	79.60	16.90	1.60
Carrots (cooked)	87.00	9.30	1.20
Parsnips (cooked)	85.00	11.30	1.30
Turnips (cooked)	91.50	5.70	1.00

vegetable; organically grown potatoes, baked in their skins and eaten with butter, are a first-class meal for anyone. They are relatively shallow rooting, so cannot be as rich in minerals as the deep-driving salsify which wins on calcium, though they hold useful quantities of both iron and phosphorus (see Table 3). Sprouting broccoli and kale are far ahead on calcium. Though spinach is fantastically richer in calcium, phosphorus and iron, it holds so much oxalic acid that it locks both minerals up as oxalates, which pass from our bodies in urine. Other members of the same family contain less oxalic acid, and spinach in moderation is of value for the other nutrients it contains. Just as we rotate our crops so we should rotate our foods, and a diet of spinach alone could kill. An American once died from eating nothing but carrots.

An average serving of vegetables is 3½ ounces (100 g), and this amount is used in all works on nutrition to calculate what every food supplies. There are a whole range of substances which lock up your vitamins and minerals. As an example, smoking uses up the body's Vitamin C, and folic acid, which is one

Table 3: MINERAL CONTENT OF POTATO AND OTHER VEGETABLES

(Dry matter)	Mg per 100 g			
	Calcium	Phosphorus	Iron	Copper
Potatoes (boiled)	4	33	0.46	0.15
Artichokes (boiled)	30	33	0.41	0.12
Beetroot (boiled)	30	36	0.70	0.14
Carrots (boiled)	46	38	0.60	0.11
Parsnips (boiled)	59	76	0.45	0.10
Radish (raw)	30	31	1.36	0.16
Salsify (boiled)	60	53	1.23	0.12
Turnips (boiled)	55	19	0.35	0.04
Broccoli (cooked)	160	54	1.52	—
Cabbage (cooked)	27	45	0.63	—
Lettuce (raw)	43	42	0.56	—
Spinach (cooked)	595	93	4.0	—

of the Vitamin B group present in leafy vegetables (also in wheatgerm), in greater quantities raw than cooked, is made unavailable by antibiotics, the contraceptive pill, a high intake of alcohol or other refined carbohydrates, and tranquillizers like Valium. A shortage of folic acid in pregnancy can cause deformities at birth, especially spina bifida. Our bodies are made to absorb all vitamins and minerals that we need from our food, and in an age of additives this is best home-grown.

Table 4 shows that every vegetable has its strong points, with peas leading on thiamine, carrots on Vitamin A, with raw spinach a good second and lettuce, broccoli and cooked spinach following closely behind. Sprouting broccoli is best of all on pantothenic acid. Those who eat plenty of vegetables, of whatever kind, are getting a first-class mixture of vitamins and minerals, with sufficient fibre to make both bran and constipation totally unnecessary.

Gardening for allergies

The ordinary healthy family, growing what they like and eating it, have no need to worry about balancing their vitamins, but there are thousands of unfortunate people who suffer from allergies and other conditions that make dieting essential for medical reasons. It is hard for those who have not experienced the acute distress of sudden allergy symptoms to understand what a difference food can make, but still harder for those who have them.

When I was a boy I played chess with a friend's father, who began by taking his queen off the board to 'make a game of it', and finished up checkmating me with only a bishop and a knight. I am a coeliac, which means that I have diarrhoea and a high temperature if I have wheat, oats, rye or barley. No bread, no biscuits, no cake, no porridge,

no beer (because of the barley), and above all no flour thickening in gravy or made-up foods. I can eat rice and maize, but for weeks I may do without them. Potatoes replace bread for me, and I manage on meat, eggs, fish, vegetables and fruit. If I were a vegetarian I should have 'lost my queen' because wholemeal bread is such an essential part of a vegetarian diet. Many coeliacs cannot take milk or dairy products, and many hay-fever sufferers, or those with constant colds or chest symptoms could well cut these out. Though this reduces calcium and riboflavin, all these can be obtained from vegetables, and it is simply a matter of eating (and growing) more of those that are high in what you are missing.

The Gluten-free Diet* (which I am on) is of considerable value to multiple-sclerosis sufferers, does not conflict with any medical treatments, and it costs less if you are able to grow your own vegetables, which replace the bought refined carbohydrate foods you do not eat, including macaroni and semolina. The real problem comes for allergy sufferers.

Rotation diets

The most unfortunate are those who have multiple allergies, and have to try and make up a nutritionally balanced diet with the few foods they can eat safely, which is like playing chess with only a bishop and a knight. Frequently they are allergic to all grains, all pulses (pea-tribe seeds and vegetables), and all milk products. They dare not just concentrate on the foods they can eat, because they would then become aller-

* A copy of the *Wholefood Gluten-free Diet* is obtainable from The Henry Doubleday Research Association, National Centre for Organic Gardening, Ryton-on-Dunsmore, Coventry CV8 3LG. Enclose a stamped addressed envelope.

Table 4: VITAMIN CONTENT OF POTATO AND OTHER VEGETABLES

Vegetable	Vitamin C	Vitamin E	Niacin	Vitamin A	Thiamine	Riboflavin	Pyridoxine	Pantothenic Acid
	Mg per 100 g			IUs	µg per 100g			
Potatoes (boiled)	10-14	0.10	1.20	20-40	100	40	320-650	220-320
Beetroot (boiled)	5	0.20	0.20	0-20	10	30	120	120
Carrots (boiled)	6	—	0.50	10,000	60	60	200	120
Parsnips (boiled)	18	—	0.20	—	80	90	—	—
Turnips (boiled)	18	0.20	0.50	—	60	60	110	37
Radish (raw)	25	—	0.10	30	40	60	—	—
Lettuce (raw)	8	—	0.20	4,000	45	45	—	110
Cabbage (raw)	150	—	0.50	150	30	50	—	180
Cabbage (cooked)	80	—	0.30	80-170	—	—	—	—
Broccoli (cooked)	100	—	0.30	3,000-5,000	139	259	—	1,100
Spinach (raw)	18	—	0.20	6,790	60	45	—	110
Spinach (cooked)	13	—	0.20	3,445	50	240	—	—
Peas (raw)	25	—	2.10	—	400	200	79-100	1,040
Peas (canned)	8	—	—	—	110	60	—	120

* An International Unit (IU) of Vitamin A is 0.0006 mg of beta-carotene, which is converted into Vitamin A in the liver.

gic to these too, so they practise a five-day rotation diet, just as gardeners rotate their crops.

The aim is to have one meat, one fruit, one carbohydrate source and one leaf vegetable daily. Allergies run by natural orders as a rule, and more people are allergic to eggs than anything else. This may well be due to an allergy to the dye that inorganic poultry feeds contain, added to give battery hens the orange yolks of free-range. Try some eggs from an organic farm or from your own birds, if you have some, as these may well be all right. Many allergy sufferers are upset by the order *Solanaceae*, which means no tomatoes, no potatoes, no aubergines and no sweet peppers. If, however, you can safely eat one member of the family, then you can probably eat the others on the same day: carrots, parsnips and parsley all on your day for the *Umbelliferae*, or artichokes and lettuce when *Compositae* are on the menu. It is to help those whose health depends on picking the right vegetables that I have brought in the numbers on the tables. Table 5 gives an example of a rotation diet. Day Two's diet indicates the problem that arises because our fruits and vegetables come from so few natural orders. It is solved by the fact that there are many which belong to natural orders to which no one (as far as we know) has ever developed allergies, probably because we do not eat them often enough to start any. New Zealand spinach in the *Aizoaceae* (1) has no relations and is

available all the summer. Others in this useful class, but available almost all the year round are lamb's lettuce (13) and miner's lettuce (10) for salads. On Day Five, salsify and scorzonera could replace or join the artichokes and lettuce because all share membership of *Compositae* (3).

Bananas are a useful carbohydrate source, but their sweetness becomes a burden as the weeks go by. Sago from the sago palm and tapioca from the cassava root (*Euphorbiacea*) are storable standbys but need supplementing with the vitamin B group, which they lack entirely. The best non-home-grown item is the sweet potato (*Ipomoea batatas*, order *Convolvulacea*) obtainable almost everywhere in shops that cater for Asians and West Indians. The pink-skinned tubers, peeled and boiled like ordinary potatoes, hold 3,500-7,000 IUs per 100 g compared with 20-30 in our simple spuds. Both share the neutrality of flavour that makes them a non-cloying daily food, unlike the decided tastes of artichokes or parsnips.

Together they put two days into a rotation diet in which tea-time bread and cake gap and the pudding problem can be solved by liquidizing the boiled tubers with as little water as possible plus grapefruit, oranges or lemons (*Rutaceae*) or berries such as thornless boysenberries or blackberries (*Rosacea*) or black- or redcurrants or gooseberries (*Saxifragacea*). The berries are best deep-frozen in small freezer bags, each bag holding enough for a single meal,

Table 5: A TYPICAL ROTATION DIET

Day One	Day Two	Day Three	Day Four	Day Five
Beef	Fish	Lamb	Pork	Chicken
Carrots (12)	Potatoes (11)	Beetroot (2)	Turnip (4)	Artichokes (3)
Parsley (12)	N.Z. Spinach (1)	Chard (2)	Cabbage (4)	Lettuce (3)
Apples	Plums	Blackcurrants	Oranges	Raspberries

either raw or cooked and rubbed through a sieve to make a seedless purée as a better way to use the redcurrant flavour.

This adds both variety and vitamins not only to allergy sufferers and those on gluten-free or grain- and milk-free diets, but those of vegans and vegetarians. The neutral taste root and fruit 'soufflé', blending carbohydrates with the vitamins and minerals for their digestion, and fruit flavours and nutritional value, in a wide range of permutations, should become as important a part of health diets as salads, but far less time and trouble to prepare. They are the organic gardener's natural convenience foods.

Rotation diets are for extreme cases, and those who have allergy symptoms should first try giving up products that could contain additives. Carrots, as an example, can take up aldrin sprayed against carrot fly, even from a field where it was last used ten years previously, and allergies work on tiny traces of substances that may affect only one person in a thousand, which can mean 56,000 sufferers in all Britain. There are plenty of best-selling books in this field, and many consultants, but do try growing more of the food you eat – the diet you dig up yourself is the safest of all.

CHAPTER 3
FOOD FOR THE SOIL

No organic gardener ever has enough compost material, for the sappy weeds of summer rot down to less than lawn-mowings and these make better compost mixed with something bulky and stemmy to add the celluloses, hemicelluloses and lignins that make lasting humus. One solution is to sow the common, striped, seeded sunflower, as sold by pet shops, 1 foot (30 cm) apart each way in March or April on any spare ground (ideally where the septic-tank overflow escapes if you have one), and let them grow 5 feet (1.50 m) high, well before they produce flower buds. Then pull them and shake the soil off their roots for composting, and sow another batch, for the seed is cheap and lasts for about three years of sowings.

With enough room, it is a good idea to add a growing-square of compost material to the rotation, which in the country can be where you empty the results of bucket sanitation (even an Elsan bucket is safe for sunflowers), and two years growing sunflowers will 'tame' the most overfed soil, such as an old chicken-run site. If the chosen area is known to be full of clubroot spores, cut off the sunflowers above the first joint, so they shoot again and give a second cutting. The stumps die off in winter, ready for a second year's sowing, and you will not have moved spore-laden roots to your compost heap which may not get hot enough to kill them all in the bulk of soil. Sweetcorn is the crop that grows the most compost material as 'spin-off' from cobs to store in the freezer for the winter. Bash their

stems with an axeback on a concrete path to speed rotting, which is cheaper and far quicker than any hand or moto-rized compost-chopper.

Cutting more compost material
Those who have transport, even a car with the back seats removed to take well-stuffed plastic sacks, can collect weeds. The rose bay willow herb, found on most waste land, is excellent and so are nettles, docks and cow parsley, mown the previous day and left to wilt which allows much more to be stuffed into the bags and means hauling less water, so you make more finished compost to the trip. Bracken is the best bargain, for it holds 2.75 per cent potash (about the same as sunflowers) when cut fresh in summer, though only about 0.2 per cent when it dies and dries rusty-brown in autumn, for the potash is returned to store in the roots by then, and if it is cut in June or July and then again in September, it will be killed out in three years. Nettles, which offer three cuts – May, July and September, and docks are also des-troyed by cuttings, but always cut be-fore they flower, so as to import no weed seeds into your garden and yet do the maximum damage to the weeds.

If you can cut quantities of cow pars-ley and hemlock (*Conicum maculatum*) on waste ground or along roadsides near your garden in May and June, you will be destroying the food supply of the carrot fly (*Psila rosea*), the onion fly (*Delia antiqua*) and the cabbage root fly (*Delia brassicae*) which feed on the pollen and nectar of the order *Umbelliferae*, which is why you should not leave run-to-seed carrots in the rows. Weed-cutting does no harm ecologically, un-like spraying hedgerows with herbicides, and the gain in compost material and pest control is worth taking free for the petrol you use collecting them.

Building compost heaps
Bulk heaps are best built as cubes like hay stacks, and they should be started with a cross-shaped trench about 6 inches (15 cm) deep and 8 inches (20 cm) wide, lined with rough wood kept in place with pegs to prevent the sides falling in. Cover the cross with brush-wood or anything that will keep the material from filling it up, then pile on your material in a layer about 1 foot (30 cm) thick in a 6 foot (2 m) square. On this, spread a layer, about 1 inch (25 mm) thick, of any organic manure, ideally pigeon, poultry, rabbit or goat. Pigeon is far the best and it is often free, for pigeon keepers know that it is 3.4 per cent nitrogen and far too strong for garden use. But it is an excellent com-post-heap 'activator' which is the source of nitrogen and phosphorus that the bacteria and fungi, which break down vegetable wastes to good humus and plant foods, must have to increase the heat of the heap to 180-190°F (65-70°C). This will cook the weed seeds like grains of rice, simmer convolvulus roots like narrow potatoes and kill dis-ease spores like a steam sterilizer.

Pile on another 8 inches to a foot (20-30 cm) thick layer and scatter on this enough garden lime to whiten the surface. The object of this is to prevent the heap becoming too acid as it will, especially if you can obtain lawn-mowings; and these can make up to half the bulk of the heap, provided they are spread through it and not left in one lump. Tennis clubs and sports grounds often have waste mowings to give away,

and so long as you do not use the grass until the second mowing after a selec-tive weedkiller has been used, they are excellent. Add another layer of material, then more activator (which makes all the difference between compost and a rubbish heap), then more material, lime again and so on until your stack is as high as it will go, which is about 5 feet (150 cm).

Slope in the sides a little, say to 4 feet (120 cm) across the flat top of a heap, 6 feet (2 m) at the base, so that it stays stable, with the open ends of the trenches extending about 6 inches (15 cm) beyond the sides and ends. The object of these trenches is to let in plenty of air, for the bacteria that make the compost need as much oxygen to produce the 180°F (65°C) temperature as if the heat had been produced by burning. Compost heaps have been de-scribed as 'bacterial bonfires', as they reduce the proportion of compounds containing carbon to those holding nit-rogen from about 70-1 to between 10-1 and 14-1. This does not leave so much bacterial food that the bacterial increase in the soil robs the crops of available nitrogen and phosphorus, which is why we make compost rather than dig the rubbish straight in.

The carpet-covered compost heap
In addition to an activator and an air supply, compost needs moisture, and something to hold this and the heat in. The cheapest way to provide these is to obtain an old carpet from a second-hand shop or a skip, and cover the heap completely. A foam-backed carpet will last for several years, but the hessian-backed type absorbs the moisture in the steam from the heap and rots down until it can itself go on the heap in about three years.

This kind of heap has the advantage that it can be made anywhere around the garden or rotated up and down its poorest portion so that all the drainings from it soak in and enrich the soil. If there is plenty of material make the heap longer, adding another cross trench every 6 feet (2 m), but keeping the same height and width. If quantities of mowings are used, or there is difficulty

in getting it to heat, set upright tomato or dahlia stakes along the trenches at 2 foot (60 cm) intervals and pull them out when it has been built, to leave extra upright air channels. A heap started in May should be ready to use by September, and can be tested by dig-

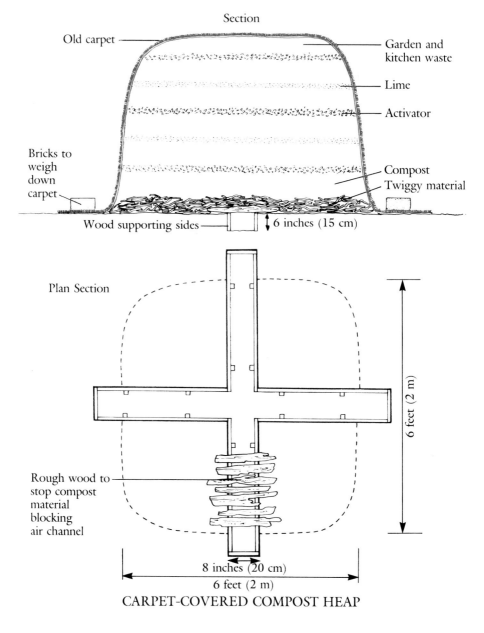

Section

Old carpet

Garden and kitchen waste

Lime

Activator

Bricks to weigh down carpet

Compost

Twiggy material

Wood supporting sides

6 inches (15 cm)

Plan Section

6 feet (2 m)

Rough wood to stop compost material blocking air channel

8 inches (20 cm)

6 feet (2 m)

CARPET-COVERED COMPOST HEAP

ging into it to see if the worms have moved in and it has become something like well-rotted manure with the plant remains showing but dark brown and easily broken. The temperature can be tested with a hot-bed thermometer, which should show a rapid rise to the required temperature in the first week, tapering off slowly until in three to four weeks it should be cold enough for the fungi to take over before the worms arrive.

The quality can be improved by turning the heap, but though this starts it heating again, it is hard work, and is unnecessary with carpet-covered heaps. Those just made in the open do not decay on the outsides which get too cold and dry, so must be turned to bring this unexpended portion of the soil's rations into the middle for consumption by the bacteria.

This system of composting is excellent with large quantities of material available at once, but most gardeners have to make their heaps little by little as compost material and kitchen waste accumulates. The original wooden New Zealand Box which stayed in one place and could last twenty years if it was well creosoted before it was nailed and bolted together can now cost almost as much as a garden shed.

Home-made wooden compost bins
Those who can find second-hand timber, or are determined to have a first-class traditional compost bin can make a standard, two-compartment model by following the diagrams and directions as given for the New Zealand Box in the HDRA leaflet *Give Up Smoking Bonfires*, of which they have already given away about 600,000.

'A box with compartments 3 feet (1 m) square to hold 1 cubic yard (0.76 m³) of finished compost in each takes 190 feet (57 m) of 4 by ½ inch (10 by 1 cm) sawn plank, six 4 foot lengths of 2 by 2 inch (5 by 5 cm) timber and five 3 foot (1 m) lengths of 2 by 1½ inch (5 by 4 cm) timber, but the dimensions are not important.

'Saw nine 6 foot (2 m) planks for the back and 27 others 3 feet (1 m) long for the sides and middle. Then creosote everything, including the uprights, and leave to dry for about a week. Other wood preservatives such as Cuprinol or Solignum can be used, but all are more expensive than creosote. If you want to paint the bin green or black, use a bitumen paint (as sold for use on corrugated iron), because it will 'take' on top of creosote, which can then replace costly undercoat with a better rot preventer.

'Lay three of the 2 by 2 inch (5 by 5 cm) uprights 3 feet (1 m) apart and nail the 6 foot (2 m) planks to the upper 3 feet (1 m) of the remaining three uprights. Dig six holes at the corners of the yard (0.91 m) squares, fit the three uprights of the back into their respective holes but replace and firm the soil round the upright only at one end. Now put the lower 1 foot (30 cm) of the upright of the first end in its hole, and nail the free ends of the planks to the upright on the back, holding a brick against it to take the shock of the hammering. Then replace the soil round the upright and firm it well.

'When the middle and other end are fitted in this way, you have a strong, wooden 'E' shape in plan. Saw the remaining planks, which make up the removable board fronts of the compartments, into lengths of slightly less than 3 feet (1 m). Fit them into slots made by nailing the last five 3 foot (1 m) lengths of 2 by 1½ inch (5 by 4 cm) sawn timber approximately ¾ inch (2 cm) from the front uprights. You will need three to make the slots on both sides of the middle divider. Creosote the front boards and their sawn ends and let them dry before fitting.

Greased bolt to hold central and back sections together

Batten nailed to back boards

Galvanized nails

Expansion restraints

Plan of central section

Front movable boards

Battens nailed to central boards

Vertical section

Carpet to release moisture and retain heat

Garden and kitchen rubbish

Lime

Activator

Coarse and stemmy material

Air channel

NEW ZEALAND BOX

'When you eventually need to move the heap, dig the soil out of the holes for the uprights as far as possible, then lift from both ends and replace in new holes dug ready 3 feet (1 m) apart on the new site. Do not try levering up the end with an iron bar, because this puts a great strain on the bin. Those who are better carpenters can nail the free ends of the 3 foot (1 m) boards to a 3 foot (1 m) length of 2 by 1 inch (5 by 2.5 cm) timber, which can be bolted to the upright with a ¼ inch (6 mm) coach bolt 4 inches (10 cm) long. Smear the bolts with motor grease or petroleum jelly before driving them through holes drilled in the uprights, the 2 by 1 inch (5 by 2.5 cm) wood and the planks from the inside, screwing the nuts on from outside, because they will be more likely to rust inside the heap. If well greased, they will screw off easily and the bin will come apart with less trouble. This is especially useful if you move house, as you can then pack your compost bin flat in the van.'

The essentials for success with this kind of heap are the air channels at the bottom (which can be trenches running from front to back of the same type used in the carpet-covered heap) and not attempting to save wood by leaving wide gaps between the planks, which lets air from the sides, destroying the draught (like holes in the sides of a chimney) and letting the heat and moisture out. There are many ready-made bins with wire sides which are utterly useless, serving only to dry the material till it is only fit to burn. Others are made

of plastic and become flimsier and flimsier as they struggle to beat the carriage problems and go by post.

Bought compost containers

There is now a better method of providing the air supply from below than the traditional bricks or trenches. Guttering for both sheds and houses is no longer made from cast iron, which needs painting, but strong grey plastic that can be easily sawn into 8-12 inch (20-30 cm) lengths. Set these hollow side down with ½ inch (13 mm) air gaps between them in place of the double rows of brick-ends protruding under the bottom boards in the front in the same way. They last indefinitely – just pick them out of the turned or finished compost for re-use again and again. It is worth buying new gutters of the large size used for houses from a builder's merchant to saw up, if short ends cannot be obtained cheaply from a builder.

Large heaps made to take quantities of mowings, cut weeds or bracken can have a network of guttering channels below, set with inch gaps to

Short sections of plastic guttering make ideal air channels for compost heaps

Guttering air channels and 'chimneys' for a large heap, shown before it is built

take dahlia stakes or stout canes. The stakes or canes are withdrawn when the heap is finished, leaving upright channels to steam like tiny chimneys through the holes you cut in the carpet covering on chilly autumn mornings. A good compost heap, heating fast in summer, can draw the flame of a match towards the ventilator channel openings.

Garden rubbish should be piled beside the compost bins to wilt and accumulate enough to cover the daily contribution from the kitchen, which should not include bones, meat scraps, or anything plastic, and only a minimum of wet paper. Layers can be thinner, 6-8 inches (16-20 cm), and the process of filling continues until the heap ceases to sink. An essential is a loam pile beside the heap, where all grass weeds with soil-packed roots should be stacked to decay slowly for potting loam, because the commonest cause of failed compost heaps is leaving too much soil on the weed roots. Once soil layers used to be added, and soil used to cover the surface, but however well the soil is shaken off the weed roots, there will always be enough left to hold a full set of soil bacteria to organize high-temperature decay.

The Californian cylinder

The Californian cylinder, invented by Captain James Macdonald (US Navy Retired), a keen organic gardener working with a poor, dry soil, is made by obtaining short lengths of pig or sheep fencing, which is square-mesh, strong, wire netting. You need lengths 9-12 feet (3-4 m) long and 3-4 feet (1-2 m) wide, so that they can be hooked together to make a cylinder about 4 feet (1.20 m) in diameter. Make the usual cross of ventilation trenches and stand the cylinder on this, tying it to stout pegs driven well in because it has a considerable sail area and could blow over

before it is fully made. Line it with opened-out cartons, sewn in place with a packing needle and twine. Then cover the channels with rough stemmy material as usual, and fill your cylinder with garden rubbish and kitchen waste.

Guttering can be set to protrude from under the carton-covered sides, radiating out from the centre where a broom stick can be driven in and then withdrawn to leave a 'chimneyhole'.

The activator used by Captain Macdonald is what is tactfully called 'Household Liquid Activator' or 'Chairman Mao's Special', because it has been used successfully in China for more than forty centuries. This is human urine, in which adults produce 13.20 g of nitrogen, 2.5 g of potassium, 1.0 g of phosphorus, 1.0 g of sulphur and 5 g of sodium every twenty-four hours. According to an organic gardening doctor, who experimented with the surplus samples from a hospital laboratory, there are no diseases likely to be passed on by urine in temperate climates (beware of Bilharzia in Africa) and the high salt level is not harmful in a compost heap, though it is enough to be appreciated by the whole beetroot family, which were originally seashore plants.

This useful free activator can be used for the compost heap, especially as an occasional tonic to speed up a slow-starting one, and as with every activator, the finished compost holds all the added minerals, which is why pigeon manure, which has 1.4 per cent phosphorus and 1.2 per cent potash as well as its generous nitrogen, is such a bargain. Four-foot (1.2 m) square versions of the carpet-covered heap are excellent for small gardens, but they do have the trouble of taking the carpet off and putting it on again after every addition, so it is best to stack the material and pile it on every few days.

Good, well-rotted manure
Manure needs entirely different treat-

ment, because its carbon-nitrogen ratio is about 20-1, even if it is strawy and fresh. The only good manure that gardeners can find today – now that farms have slurry tanks and tankers rather than yards and dung-carts – is from riding stables or individual horse owners who have used straw litter. Peat is second best, but shavings litter manure is useless, because the carbon-nitrogen ratio of shavings is 500-1 and the damage it can do to a soil lasts for years.

To convert raw manure from a stable to well-rotted 'real good stuff' in four to six weeks, build a heap about 4 feet (1.2 m) wide and high, tapered in to about 30 inches (75 cm) across the top, and as long as the load needs, and whack it firm with the flat of the spade. It is best built on a sheet of 500-gauge polythene, to collect the drainings which would otherwise be wasted, folded up at the sides and ends and held up with stakes. Then cover it with a second sheet, weighed down all round with heavy wood or stones to stop the wind tearing it away. The best polythene for this purpose is dicarded from commercial growers' polythene tunnels, because it is free and semi-opaque from the action of sunlight (which is why it is discarded).

The steam from the heating fresh manure condenses on the underside of the sheet, especially at night, and prevents further heating, while lack of air stops continued breakdown. This is the reverse of composting, for the object is to take the straw a stage or two further along the road to humus, to 'tame' the fierce fresh nitrogen and to preserve the

Sew carpet to pig fencing with string and packing needle

Supporting pegs

Wood-lined air channels 6 inches (15 cm) wide and deep

CALIFORNIAN CYLINDER COMPOST BIN

plant foods until they are needed, by a process more like silage-making than composting. The system removes the risk of 'firefang' fungus which invades manure heaps with a white mycelium that wastes both nitrogen and humus. In the past the heap would be spread, watered with brine and restacked, but the polythene system saves us this trouble.

Dealers are often keen to sell pig manure, because farmers know that the copper sulphate they mix in the feed for faster fattening will build up to toxic levels in the soil and stay there. Organic farmers who do not use copper or other additives never sell their manure. They value their fertility, so it is only the inorganic who sell manure and buy chemicals instead. Manure from cows is safe but sloppy, even with straw, and it pays to buy baled straw and add an extra 20 per cent to increase the humus, unless they have been generously littered. The polythene process will convert it all to better manure than you can ever buy.

The only manure that may even be delivered free today, is that from riding schools or stables where the litter is a mixture of shavings and short ends from woodworking factories. This costs the stable owners about twice as much as baled straw and gives them a disposal problem they may have to solve by burning their manure with a special oil-fired burner, instead of selling their strawy manure to mushroom growers or gardeners at good prices. This is not due to stupidity but the fact that horses can be allergic to some of the nine different chemicals that are sprayed on wheat straw today. They may have bought from the same inorganic farmer for years and then one of his herbicides, fungicides or pesticides will develop a resistant variety of weed, pest or disease and he will try the latest remedy. Then perhaps half a dozen of the most costly

and highly bred horses will develop allergy symptoms; the baffled (and experienced) vet will advise changing the litter and the trouble vanishes, leaving the owner with a manure problem instead. Shavings litter horse manure is safe only on the surface, used like bark as a weed-suppressing mulch under shrubs, where it is excellent, but never dig it in.

Those who have never suffered from allergies often insist that people without enough to do imagine their symptoms, ignoring the fact that the chemical revolution of the past fifteen years has invaded the kitchen more than any other room in the house. Husbands generally get away with relatively little exposure to these domestic chemicals but wives usually have to live with it. Horses are having to live with it too and, however intelligent they are, no one has ever seen them reading books on allergies and yet they still suffer from allergies and the symptoms are only too real.

Autumn leaf humus
Dead leaves are the most wasted source of lasting humus today, and in most towns and suburbs it is possible to obtain an extra supply, either unofficially by bribing the roadmen, or officially through the council. Ratepayers are entitled to have the benefit of the leaves that their rates have paid to be swept, instead of paying to have them burnt, releasing dangerous air pollution. Write to your local paper and make a row, for 5 cubic yards (3.8 m^3) of leaves as swept, stack to three, and rot to two, which is roughly a ton. This is rather richer in plant foods than peat and far cheaper, even if the roadmen in your area are greedy, and its help in holding moisture on sandy soils and lightening heavy clays goes on for years.

A traditional leafmould heap can go in dry shade under trees where nothing much will grow. Level the ground and drive in stout posts 3 feet (1 m) high at the corners, adding extra posts every yard (0.9 m) if you are going to have leaves enough to make a large heap. Staple 3 foot (0.91 m) high wire netting to the outsides of the posts and pile in the leaves as they are gathered, removing dead branches and paper litter if they are swept from the streets. Hose the heap once or twice the first summer, especially if this is a dry one.

Never include weeds or garden rubbish in the leaf pile (or dead leaves in a compost heap), for the decay of leaves is carried out by fungi that need no oxygen because there is very little heating, and the whole process is much slower. After a year the heap will have sunk and firmed, so the posts can be dug up with the netting and moved to make the enclosure for next autumn's leaves. Year old leafmould is good enough to dig into a sandy soil or to lighten clays, but for potting soil it should wait for another year.

Hastened leafmould heaps

There is a legend that plane and chestnut leaves are 'poisonous' and will not decay, though if this was true there would be seams of coal-like unrotted leaves built up through the centuries of chestnut coppices that grow the hop poles of Kent. They merely need more time, and there are two ways round the problem. Start with a 9 foot (2.7 m) length on 3 feet (1 m) wide wire netting and hook the ends together as though making a California Cylinder. There is no need to dig air channels, because no oxygen is needed; just staple it upright to a stout post, fill it with well-trodden leaves, and pour Household Liquid Activator on them. This will break down refractory leaves in one year rather than three, and produces improved decay for leaves of any kind. This should really be called a 'Peggy Pile' after Dr Peggy Ellis of the HDRA, the inventor of the method.

Another system begins with a traditional leaf stack, but in the spring, as soon as ample lawn-mowings are available, turn the leaf stack, mixing in about 25 per cent of its bulk of the mowings. This distributes the mowings among the leaves, where they decay with the help of the leafmould-making fungi, which are evidently delighted with their new diet, for again they will produce good leafmould in as little as six months. This is neither leafmould nor compost, free from weed seeds because there should be none in spring mowings, and none among the leaves, making an excellent surface coat to go between bush fruit, or as a mulch for no-digging gardeners.

Leaf humus without heaps

The head gardeners of the past valued leafmould for its lasting qualities, and when they had to *buy* it insisted on oak or beech because this had its plant foods the most firmly locked up by tannins. Otherwise they used leafmould made from every leaf on the estate, for peat has been used for barely fifty years as an ingredient for every potting soil. Because it has so little rapidly rottable carbohydrates, dead leaves do not rob the soil of nitrogen and phosphorus, so those who have a new garden full of raw subsoil can spread raw, dead leaves even 6 inches (15 cm) thick on the surface and have them spread through the top 8 inches (20 cm) or so with a powerful Rotavator, which chops them and distributes them through the surface layer. Give two cultivations, and before the second one spread as much as 1 pound a square yard (500 g per 0.84 m^2) of lime to correct acidity. The cost of hiring the machine and operator will be far less than having any gardener dig in the leaves, and it will add *enough* humus material to make a real difference.

Organic lawn care

A field on a Norfolk organic farm has been under permanent pasture for over 250 years – the only fertilizer being the dung from the cattle grazing there and enough lime to keep up the calcium. Calcium is the mineral demanded in greatest quantity for milk and bones and it also keeps the soil (which has built up nearly three feet (90 cm) of dark, humus-rich surface layer after centuries of good farming) neutral (pH 7), which is what earthworms prefer, unlike the worms that are found in dung, compost and leafmould heaps, which need acid conditions.

It is to earthworms that this field owes its fertility, both the ordinary *Lumbricus terrestris* and the deeper digging *Allolobophora nocturna* that comes up at night to gather the grass the cattle have spilt from their munching mouths. More than 100 tonnes of soil a year pass through the digestions of the 3¾ million earthworms usually present in two and a half acres (1 hectare). There it is ground by small stones in their gizzards, acted on by their digestive enzymes and thoroughly mixed with broken down organic matter. An American comparison between wormcasts from a pasture and soil samples from the same field after ploughing, showed 150 parts per million of available phosphoris in the casts and only 20 parts per million in the soil, with 358 parts per million potash in the casts against 32 parts per million in the samples.

Earthworms live up to three years, barring being eaten by birds, moles and other predators, and their bodies are 72 per cent protein. The nitrates from these and their excretions add up to the equivalent of 478.5 pounds of nitrate of soda per two and a half acres (1 hectare) per year. The difference between the chemical and the concentrated contribution from the worms is that this is released slowly under the conditions of temperature and moisture for the plants to take it as they need it without wasting any in the drainage like the chemicals causing pollution in our drinking water that are harmful to health, especially for babies.

The organic gardener's lawn is his own 'permanent pasture' and he 'grazes' it with his mower, taking off crop after crop of the ideal mulching material for use under bush fruit or between shrubs, in the compost heap and in the trenches for maincrop potatoes to provide the acidity that reduces scab. Unfortunately, mowers leave no manure, but by taking off the grass box we can duplicate the effect of cows eating untidily.

We can improve the 'down-take' of the worms that are farming our lawns by liming to reduce the acidity caused by letting the mowings lie. Start with 8 oz a square yard (240 g per m^2) of slaked lime, ideally using a simple soil testing kit that shows whether the pH of your soil is neutral or not. Take at least six widely spaced soil samples with an apple corer and mix them well to get a true reading. Wait a fortnight and try again, reliming if the pH value is still too low.

Break up and spread the casts your pro-worm policy will bring with a stiff broom, also your tealeaves which the worms will convert into lasting humus and extra plant foods replacing the missing manure. It is possible to get spent teabags free from friendly cafés to scatter thickly on the lawn and break up by running the mower over them (set low), which tosses the empty bags out through the grass box opening for the brooms to brush up. Rotted leafmould, especially the 'hastened' versions, is also excellent, and 8 ounces a square yard (240 g per m^2) of fine bonemeal spread in April or May on really hungry lawns, that are growing moss as a protest against an uncaring society that mows away everything and puts nothing back, works wonders.

Liming your lawn to achieve a neutral pH of 7 discourages moss but encourages clover, which to organic gardeners is not a weed but a good source of nitrogen, though it causes dangerous slipperiness on tennis courts. Rosette weeds that miss the mower such as flat thistles and dandelions can be killed individually by putting a level teaspoonful of salt on their crowns. This is tedious but very effective. Those whose lawns are desperately weedy can mix ten parts, by weight, of dry sand, seven of sulphate of ammonia and three of sulphate of iron, to make an old-fashioned lawnsand that was good enough for Wisley in the 1920s! Scatter this at the rate of 4-6 oz a square yard (110-160 g per m^2) in spring where the weeds are thickest. It is a good killer for daisies, pearlwort and suckling clover, but, unfortunately, for white clover, too. It leaves no residues in the mowings unlike selective weed-killer.

Under the carpet

A great many allotment sites are dying of 'vacant plot disease' as members, especially members of the Committees, for whatever reason, stop working on the allotments and new members are not attracted. It is therefore possible for wouldbe organic gardeners in flats or with tiny gardens to take on even three or four allotments very easily. Start by hiring a rough grass mower to run over the once cultivated allotment and its surrounding paths to rake up for 'hay' or a first compost heap. There will be plenty of choice so ask any surviving plot-holder which plots have been empty longest, and pick these, because nine to twelve years' vacancy gives time for the clubroot spores to have died of old age.

Then go round the local carpet shops that advertise a free fitting service as they have to take away the old carpets and are likely to want to just give them away. Spread these on the mown surfaces overlapping them well at the edges, and 'stitching' them down through the overlaps with giant wire 'staples'. These can be made with bought galvanized wire, but it is far cheaper to save the free wire coathangers that you are given when you have clothes dry-cleaned, or to buy these by the dozen very cheaply from an Oxfam shop. Use them generously for it is important not to have the carpets tearing and flapping with the wind underneath, as they will do if they are not held firmly.

The carpets can be put into place through autumn and winter, especially if the object is to reclaim a large area for an organic gardeners' club, but all must be in place by March. In this month and April the wireworms (*Agriotes* species, there are five) will be turning into click beetles and flying off to lay eggs that will become the familiar light brown larvae that can slaughter the first potato crops on new allotments. These beetles cannot get out through the carpets and, as the dead and dying grass roots will have fed them well, a record number of the 500,000 an acre old pastures average, will be killed off. If they are known to be a real pest in your area, it could pay to wait for a second April and another kill, then start cropping with French and runner beans, Brussels sprouts and winter vegetables to be followed by potatoes in the third spring.

There will be very great earthworm activity under the carpet, with plenty of energy food in the dead couch grass to drive them deep and far, bringing subsoil minerals into circulation and taking up the nitrogen fixed by the free-living bacteria (many more than in pea-tribe roots) also feeding on the grass roots. After a year, when the carpets come off, the ground will be relatively easily dug,

Coathangers adapted to hold down carpets to kill weeds

but the concentrated bonus from the earthworms will be near the surface, so do not dig it all in deep.

The quickest and easiest method is to hire a Rotovator and have the cleared ground tilled twice 4-6 inches (10-15 cm) deep, put in your potatoes, keeping them well earthed up, and hoe off as many crops of germinated weed seeds as you can, for the weeds that seeded themselves before the grass took over will be waiting.

The 'no-digging' system aims at keeping all the weeds safely underground. Spread strips of compost or well-rotted manure and set the seed tubers on them. Then cover with 3-4 inches (7-10 cm) of hay (which should be cut and dried before the weeds in it flower) or old straw, which can often be got from a left-over stack of bales. When the potato shoots are through the first layer, work in another round them, and finally cover with a thick layer of lawn mowings to exclude the light and prevent them from turning green.

Green potatoes contain the alkaloid solanine, which can produce distressing gastric upsets. At lifting time, turn back the mulch and pick the potatoes off the surface.

Apart from the problem of using inorganic farm straw, and the fact that the system produces quantities of small potatoes compared with traditional methods, no-digging means less heavy work but more hoeing. It also conserves compost, for the sheet that is made under the potatoes lasts three other squares of the rotation, so there is no wheeling, no turning and no bin filling and emptying. When you dig, you let air into the soil that breaks down the compost faster. Many organic gardeners are fiercely for it, others oppose it and both are right, for everyone has the right to garden how he or she likes in his or her own garden or allotment.

The carpet system is also new and hundreds of gardeners will find out how best to use the new system that is based on successful organic farming tech-

Above Composting involves many micro-organisms. Many need air and a supply of air from the bottom, often through brick-lined channels, provides the oxygen for the bacterial bonfire that recycles our rubbish.

Below Timber for traditional compost bins is now expensive. This type, made with short ends or wire pig fencing, lined with open cartons, keeps the wind out and the heat and moisture in for the minimum cost.

Bottom Sunflower seeds, cheap from pet shops, grows good compost material if you pull the plants up before they flower. Older stems, brassica stumps and sweetcorn stalks compost better if you spread them on your garage driveway and crush them with your tyres.

Above Dead leaves, stacked tall and tidy behind wire netting, rot to form lasting humus. Do not mix the leaves with weeds as they decay mainly with the help of forest fungi – a separate process needing no activator.

In dry autumns, hose freshly stacked leaves to start them decaying fast with the leftover energy from summer. Though oak and beech last longest in the soil, all leaves but those of conifers and evergreens make leafmould.

Left A 6 inch (15cm) layer of freshly swept leaves, Rotavated into even raw subsoil in new gardens, with 1 pound a square yard (455 g per 0.83 m²) of slaked lime, starts the humus-building process cheaply and fast.

Below Fresh, strawy manure should be stacked firmly under black or clear polythene, weighed down so it does not get blown away, and in six summer weeks you will have the 'well rotted manure' of the past that used tarpaulin as a covering before the age of plastic.

niques. Its immediate value lies in offering a cheap and easy way of reclaiming the derelict allotments that are a national scandal.

Lime, the soil sweetener

The best lime for everyone is ordinary garden lime, because though ground limestone, which is calcium carbonate, lasts longer in the soil, it is used by farmers, and therefore hard to buy in small quantities. Garden, or 'slaked', lime is very fine grains of calcium hydroxide which act quickly, for example in lowering the acidity of a compost heap to help the bacteria that produce rapid heating. Because there is so much carbonic acid excreted by the roots of all plants and weeds, it becomes calcium carbonate by a chemical reaction in the soil, while compost-heap bacteria are also producing carbonic acid in quantity, so there is no problem.

Minerals that matter

Ground dolomitic limestone, which is half calcium carbonate and half magnesium carbonate, is used instead of lime at about 8 oz a square yard (220 g per 0.83 m^2), for tomato borders or anywhere that a previous gardener has used quantities of potash fertilizers. These fertilizers lock up magnesium, making the lower leaves of tomato plants turn yellow while the veins stay green, a condition also seen in raspberries and other crops, and usually mistaken for a virus instead of the consequence of too many chemicals. One dressing is usually enough, though inorganic gardeners who still go on piling on the potassium would need it every other year. It can be obtained from the HDRA if you fail to find it locally.

So can rock potash, or Adularian shale, mined in Scotland, which is 8-10 per cent potassium, far more readily available than in the basalt, feldspar, and granite used in Europe. It lasts in the soil without washing out like chemical fertilizers and is ideal for the gardener who wants to grow gooseberries on a poor sandy soil. Clays usually have enough potassium, waiting for the roots to pick out, but rock potash at about 8 oz a square yard (220 g per 0.83 m^2) is an organic answer for all potash-hungry crops, especially potatoes.

The accepted division between organic fertilizers and the mineral sources that can be used where a soil is short of an essential plant food is to allow fine-ground, natural rock particles which are what roots normally find in the soil, or which soil bacteria or fungi can make available to them. A soluble chemical fertilizer, like nitrate of soda, muriate and sulphate of potash and superphosphate washes from the soil and is taken up directly by the plant, with a number of consequences to flavour and pest and disease resistance. A classic example is Kainite, from the dried-up sea-salt at Stassfurt in Germany, which is a mixture of potassium, magnesium and sodium chlorides, used for sugar beet by inorganic farmers in Britain, and regarded as 'organic' in Europe, because it is not 'refined' but used as it is dug. In Israel they have the Dead Sea, with much the same mixture of salts, but these are sorted out and the potassium chloride is sold separately. Potatoes, unlike people, do not consider a chemical organic if it comes from Germany, and inorganic if from Israel, and grow with that undesirable 'inorganic' flavour that every organic gardener knows when he runs out of home-grown and has to buy from a greengrocer.

Ground minerals for heavy clays

Today's new houses on heavy clays have sites cleared and smeared by machinery until the gardens are puddled into putty, while lawns on clays continuously mown with heavy mowers, unlike the light, hand machines of the past, pack down the soil so hard they they grow moss in spite of spiking with a special roller gadget. Many proprietary preparations are sold for lightening clays that include filler material like brick dust, but the cheapest and most effective is a mixture of 20 per cent horticultural dolomitic limestone and 80 per cent gypsum (which is calcium sulphate), plus traces of other minerals because it is quarried and ground as a natural rock.

The properties of clay that gardeners hate as they heave up the heavy forkfulls every autumn in the faint hope that frost will make easier digging, are too complex to describe, though a model of the process looks like an explosion in a billiard ball factory. It can be demonstrated by stirring some of your stickiest clay into two glasses of water. Stir a teaspoonful of gypsum into one and leave the other without. If you wait and watch you will see all the suspended clay gathers into small crumbs and falls to the bottom, leaving clear water, while the glass without gypsum stays as cloudy as ever. Adding the dolomite, as well as adding magnesium, has a catalytic effect, helping the action of the gypsum in breaking up the clay.

Spread 12 oz a square yard (400 g per 0.83 m^2) and hoe it into your clay in autumn or spring or both, with the second season showing a real change in the texture of the soil. It will not be quick, but the effect can be watched as the soil colour changes and the puddles between the vegetable rows vanish as the water gets away again. The mixture is no substitute for humus, but the air supply to the roots and the soil bacteria is improved, making plant foods already in the clay available to the plants and there is a bonus in fertility, turning heavy clays into soils to be appreciated rather than hated. Regular dressings of

2-3 ounces a square yard (60-90 g per 0.83 m^2) will maintain the improvement, and as dolomite, which is widely used by Continental organic farmers and gardeners, and gypsum, are no more expensive than ordinary lime, they are easily affordable. For clay lawns apply the mixture at the same rate as for bare ground in the autumn and let the worms take it under as a supplement to nature's lawn food, which is wormcasts.

Wood ashes

Wood ashes are used by most organic gardeners, but the potash here, which is mainly potassium carbonate, washes out just as badly as chemical sources from the sandy soils that need it. They vary widely from 37 per cent potash for lime-tree branch ashes to 8 per cent for oak and birch, but they are also rich in calcium, with spruce up to 60 per cent and elm down to 17 per cent, so their best use is scattered, in place of lime, on compost-material layers, where there will be some complex chemical reactions, one of which produced the saltpetre (potassium nitrate) that made the first gunpowder for the Chinese in 350 BC. Do not try to use up the ashes from a wood-burning stove with extra thick layers in the compost heap, or you will unbalance it chemically. Spread your ashes on the floor of the poultry house under the perches, and they will dry out the droppings until these can be swept rather than scraped out, with a real saving in trouble, time and smell. There is a chemical reaction between the alkaline potassium carbonate, and the acid ammonium carbonate of the poultry manure, and the result is as shown in Table 6. The potassium is converted to a less readily available form, and the result is a far better balanced manure than anything else from the poultry shed. Keep the grey-brown powder in a dry place, and use it as a good general organic fertilizer at the rate of 4-8 oz a square yard (110-220 g per 0.83m^2). It is worth keeping chickens, if you have a wood stove, to get the fertilizer.

Table 6: POULTRY MANURE, BEFORE AND AFTER MIXING WITH WOOD ASH

	Fresh droppings %	Wood ash treated %
Moisture	72.00	16.70
Organic matter	20.00	89.85
Nitrogen	1.66	0.90
Phosphorus	0.91	1.50
Potash	0.48	2.12

Organic fertilizers

Though there is a slowly released source of phosphorus in rock phosphate, which is fossilized dead fish from dried-up seabeds mainly in North Africa, and Gafsa rock phosphate is bought in quantities by organic farmers, no gardeners have any need to use it, because fine bonemeal is easy to buy and offers both phosphorus and nitrogen. There are a number of organic fertilizers of this type which are relatively expensive, including dried blood, which pro-vides the tonic effect of quickly released nitrogen, for a crop that has hung about too long; hoof and horn meal, offering slowly released nitrogen; and blood, fish and bonemeal, which is, today, material from slaughter houses and fish-finger factories, that cannot go into cattle cake. The quantities to use will be quoted in the month-by-month chapters, but gardeners really need them less often than they may think they do. Table 7 gives details of the chemical comparison between these fertilizers.

Table 7: AVERAGE ANALYSIS OF ORGANIC FERTILIZERS

	Moisture (per cent)	Nitrogen (per cent)	Phosphorus (per cent)	Potash (per cent)
Dried blood	—	9-13	0.8	—
Hoof and horn meal	—	6.5-13.2	0.1-0.2	—
Bonemeal	0.2-14	0.3-4.6	14.1-33.2	—
Bone and meatmeal	6.0	3.9-12.3	0.9-19.0	—
Fish meal	—	6.3-8.9	6.0-8.9	—
Seaweed meal	—	2.80	0.22	2.29

Seaweed is an excellent tomato fertilizer as it holds more potash than phosphorus. There are many liquid seaweed preparations for use as 'foliar feeds', for plants feed not only through their roots, but their leaves as well. This was discovered during World War II, when our blockade prevented the French importing copper sulphate for spraying their vines, so they used copper nitrate instead, and discovered they were curing the symptoms of nitrogen deficiency.

Seaweed contains an almost complete set of trace elements, including boron, bromine, calcium, copper, iodine, magnesium, manganese and sodium, all in forms that leaves can take in readily. All plants, but especially trees, throw away unwanted minerals through their leaves, and take what they want as it goes by, so if the leaves of any crop are strangely discoloured, or trees show the colours of autumn at the wrong season, try using seaweed sprays on the leaves. You will not know what the shortage was, but this does not matter – if the trouble has stopped that is good enough.

Soil testing

A soil-testing kit is of little value to an organic gardener, because it merely counts the loose change in the pockets of his garden, and ignores its investments and bank account. The reliable test is for lime, and this consists of a kind of liquid litmus paper which is poured into a small scoop with a sample of soil, and a colour chart that shows the pH level and how much lime is needed to bring it to between pH 6.5 and pH 7.0 which is neutral and the level at which most garden vegetables and fruit will thrive.

The shortage all sandy soils may have is potassium, because heavy liming and dressings of phosphorus can lock the potash out of root reach on clays, and on sands, chemical potash salts wash away. Gooseberries show potassium deficiency when the leaves turn a rather blue-green colour, have light-brown bands round the edges and fall early; tomatoes also have light-brown scorching at the leaf edges, and the fruit ripens patchily, with green and yellow areas merging into red, instead of changing from green to red shade by

shade, while potato leaves turn bronzy green with brown spots between the veins and foliage dying down too soon for a good crop. Broad, French and runner beans show light-brown leaf-edge scorching, as do beetroot, cabbage and lettuce.

The cure for what is usually taken to be some deadly virus or new disease is rock potash, which can be scattered between the growing plants, for unlike a chemical fertilizer it will not scorch the foliage and takes time to act. Fork the powder lightly in during the summer and there should be no trouble the following year. Wood ashes can be used for quick action, but remember that they vary. Twigs have most and apple prunings burn to make an ash worth saving for emergencies.

Comfrey for fertility

The best source of quickly available potassium for organic gardeners is comfrey, and everyone should have a comfrey bed to supply a very useful high-potash liquid manure, for tomatoes setting their first fruit and other potash-hungry plants. This powerful, long-lived perennial, which is also a good food, a fodder crop and a valuable medicinal herb, needs a position in full sun away from trees or privet hedges, so its roots can go down deeply to gather minerals far out of reach of most garden plants.

Comfrey rarely sets seed and is grown from offsets, which are short sections of root each with a growing point which should be just below the surface when they are planted 2 feet (60 cm) apart each way at any time of year except between November and the end of January, when the roots are entirely dormant and there may be losses in hard weather. Otherwise comfrey is fully hardy. It is a natural hybrid which took place in Upland, Sweden, between *Symphytum officinale*, the herbalist's comfrey, and *S. asperum*, the blue-flowered prickly comfrey from Russia, so the modern mixtures are correctly called *S. uplandicum*.

They were sorted out at the HDRA Trial Ground at Bocking, and the usual garden varieties are Bocking 14, with thin stems and mauve flowers, which will grow 3 feet (0.9 m) high if left uncut, and is the highest in potash, and Bocking 4, which has thick, solid stems, large leaves and flowers nearer to violet in colour. This has a higher yield, starts growing rather later in the spring, and is grown in many countries as stock feed. Its leaves are used as a green vegetable, but they are not particularly attractive, and the major uses of the plant today are as a source of liquid manure and as a dried herbal tea mainly used to alleviate arthritis.

Starting and keeping comfrey

The essential first step to starting a comfrey bed is to search out all the roots of perennial weeds, for it is a permanent garden feature like an asparagus bed, but much more lasting. Dig in manure to give it a start, and after planting hoe betwen the rows to kill out annual weeds and especially grass. The best planting times are March, April and May, or in September, which gives them time to become well established before winter. Summer plantings do well if they are watered well after planting and during the week that follows.

Spring-planted comfrey should be cut with shears about 2 inches (5 cm) above the ground in July or August, to prevent it flowering the first season, and this provides enough foliage for a trial of its qualities as a liquid manure. Leave further growth to die down in the plant in October and build up strength for a full cutting programme the following year. This begins with a first cut in April and the last in late September or early October, roughly every six weeks,

which means four or five cuts a year.

After a comfrey bed has been planted for two years, it can be increased very simply by driving a spade through these established plants about 3 inches (7 cm) below the surface in March when the growing points are just showing. Lift off the crowns of the plants and cut them up into sections of root, each with a growing point, to replant where required. Do the cutting up over a spread newspaper (for though comfrey rarely seeds, every fragment of root will grow), fold up the paper and dump it in the dustbin. A weed is a plant in the wrong place and carelessly scattered comfrey can be an awkward weed.

If you are extending the comfrey bed, fill in the holes with soil, and wait for the decapitated plants to grow again, missing two cuts but becoming rather more productive next season. If, however, you planted them in what you now feel is the wrong place, spread about a ¼ of an ounce (7 g) of ammonium sulphate (the safest known weedkiller) on the cut surface of the roots left in the ground. This will destroy them completely, and in about four weeks the chemical becomes sulphate of ammonia, which is a common chemical fertilizer and washes harmlessly from the soil. It can be used to kill swarms of small comfrey plants where a Rotavator has been used in an attempt to kill comfrey, or where it has been dug out, leaving the soil full of fragments. Stir 1 pound (455 g) of the white crystals into a gallon (4.5 litres) of water and apply with a rosed can over a 10 foot (3 m) square area. In eight weeks any crop can be sown or planted after it.

This total weedkiller can be used to destroy horseradish and other awkward weeds, but it is comparatively expensive, and no organic gardener likes using chemicals. This substance is, roughly speaking, sulphate of ammonia made crooked, and the greedier a weed is for nitrogen the more it takes, which is why it should only be used when weeds are growing strongly, never in autumn or winter. It kills not by poison but by bad diet – like killing rats by feeding them only white bread and white sugar. In eight weeks you can plant or sow any crop on the treated area. It is never poisonous to birds or pets, and it produces an *increase* in the worm population after use.

When the plants die down completely, dig between the rows to take out any perennial weeds, and lime if necessary. Once a comfrey bed is established and growing well, there is little need to hoe because the foliage meets in a solid mass, suppressing annual weeds. Because it is producing more than a hundredweight (50.80 kg) of foliage a season, comfrey needs generous feeding. Always give it manure on the surface in spring – ideally deep-litter poultry manure, with straw or peat litter – spread as a 2 inch (5 cm) thick surface coat; pigeon manure is excellent and so is sewage sludge. Because it is not a legume (it belongs to the *Boraginaceae*, the anchusa or forget-me-not family) and has no bacterial helpers fixing the nitrogen that gives it remarkably high protein, it needs plenty of manure, but can take it very crude. Fresh poultry manure or Household Liquid Activator which you cannot use direct on other crops will keep it growing to produce a very much better organic fertilizer than the manure you give it.

The garden uses of comfrey

It has a carbon-nitrogen ratio of 9.8-1, so it is a kind of 'instant compost'; when wilted overnight to concentrate it, and spread along the bottom of maincrop potato trenches at the rate of 1½ pounds a foot (680 g per 0.3 m) of row in place of lawn mowings it lowers the potato scab rate as well as producing excellent crops of first-class flavour, becaue of its very high level of immediately available organic potash. Table 8 shows the comparative analysis of wilted comfrey, compost and farmyard manure.

The analysis figures given in Table 10 for dried comfrey show why Bocking 14 is the favourite for fertility with about a third more potash than Bocking 4, making it rather bitter to eat as a vegetable and unattractive to rabbits, while the wild *S. officinale* has the least of all. The carpeting comfrey *S. grandiflorum*, with its larger, white, bell flowers hanging from short, thin stems in May, contains little potassium, and no allantoin, the medicinal principle which has earned comfrey the name of 'knitbone' and 'wound heal' in all the languages of Europe.

The problem of using comfrey in potato trenches is that in cold springs there may not be enough bulk grown in

Table 8: COMPARATIVE ANALYSIS OF WILTED COMFREY, COMPOST AND FARMYARD MANURE

Material	Nitrogen Water (per cent)	Phosphorus (N) (per cent)	Potash (P_2O_5) (per cent)	Carbon- (K_2O) (per cent)	Nitrogen ratio
Farmyard manure	76.0	0.64	0.23	0.32	14:1
Russian comfrey (wilted)	75.0	0.74	0.24	1.19	9.8:1
Compost	76.0	0.50	0.27	0.81	10:1

Table 9: COMPARATIVE ANALYSIS OF COMFREY AND TWO
COMMERCIAL LIQUID FEEDS

	Tomorite (per cent)	Marinure (per cent)	Comfrey (per cent)
Dry matter	0.1410	0.0480	0.4090
Nitrogen	0.0130	0.0070	0.0140
Potash	0.0139	0.0019	0.0340
Phosphorus	0.0093	0.0001	0.0059

time for earlies. It is, however, better to leave potatoes chitting rather longer in a cold season so they wait for the comfrey, and to lay the long, sprouted seed tubers flat on the surface of the wilted comfrey, which heats a little and warms them ahead.

Comfrey's most popular use today is as a liquid manure. This is made in two ways. The first is to put 14 pounds (6.3 kg) of freshly cut comfrey in a 20 gallon (9.92 l) fibreglass waterbutt (metal drums rust and add toxic quantities of iron oxide to the liquid manure), fill up with rain or tap water, replace the lid to exclude the light, and in about four weeks a clear liquid can be drawn from the tap at the bottom. A comparison between this and commercial liquid feeds made up according to the manufacturer's directions is given in Table 9. Tomorite is a popular inorganic tomato feed, and Marinure an organic one based on seaweed.

The comfrey liquid has three times as much potassium, a third less phosphorus and rather more nitrogen than the other two, which is why it is ideal for tomatoes, onions, gooseberries, beans and all potash-demanding crops. Because the liquid is clear it can also be used as a foliar feed, and will not block a watering-can rose when it is applied generously as a tonic.

The disadvantage of this system is that comfrey foliage is about 3.4 per cent protein, and when proteins break down they smell. The answer is to use a plastic cask or a metal drum, well coated with black bitumen paint inside and out, and bore a hole in the side just above the bottom. Stand the container on bricks or stout wood so it is high enough off the ground to allow a dish to go under it. Fill the container with cut comfrey, packing it solid and put-

Table 10: COMPARATIVE ANALYSIS OF DRIED COMFREY,
BOCKING 4 AND BOCKING 14

	Bocking 4 (per cent)	Bocking 14 (per cent)	S. officinale (per cent)
Calcium	2.35	2.77	1.31
Phosphoric acid	1.25	0.75	0.72
Potassium	5.04	7.09	3.09
Iron	0.253	0.144	0.098
Manganese p.p.m.	137	133	85
Cobalt	trace	trace	—

ting something heavy like a lump of concrete on the surface. In about three weeks, a black liquid will drip from the hole into the dish to collect and dilute with 4 fluid ounces of the concentrate to a gallon of water (115 ml concentrate to 4.5 l). The concentrate can be stored in a screwtop bottle if you do not want to use it immediately. The analysis averages:

Nitrogen (N)   0.11 per cent
Phosphorus (P)0.06 per cent
Potassium (K) 0.55 per cent

If this mixture is to be used as a foliar feed, it should be filtered through a pair of old tights, because it will contain fine particles that may block the syringe. The residue of comfrey left in the bottom of the container when the black liquid ceases to drip is good compost and can be tipped out and dug in before the container is refilled for another charge. The process can be hastened by pouring some urine in to give a high nitrogen start and some extra potassium.

Comfrey foliage holds far more carbohydrate and protein than fibre, which is why it is a good pig food but a poor compost material. It can be used to add more plant foods, and even as an activator, but it rots down to very little compared with high-fibre material such as sunflower stems. So use the surplus mixed in with other material. The liquid-manure methods waste less of the nitrogen. It is of greater value as a surface coat, spread between tomato plants or under soft fruit, especially gooseberries. Here it can be covered with lawn mowings (which should not be in contact with the stems of the mulched crop), which will speed its decay into a kind of surface-made compost, from which plant foods will wash down into the soil below.

Making comfrey tea
Though comfrey leaves can be used direct to make tea in summer, it is more convenient to dry them for use round the year. Pick the largest mature leaves you can find, and lay them on small-mesh wire-netting in the sun, so they have free circulation of air below them as well as above. When they are floppy and drying at the edges, finish them off in an electric oven turned low and with the door open to let out the steam. Crush them when crisp and store in a screwtop jar. Comfrey tea is usually mixed with equal parts of ordinary tea and about six cups a day has kept away the pain of arthritis for thousands of people who are convinced that it is the finest medicinal herb of all.

CHAPTER 4
JANUARY

January is the month without outdoor sowing or planting, when food depends on stored roots, what is frozen or bottled and what can still be dug or picked in the garden. Salads that can be cut quickly even under cleared snow are lamb's lettuce, miner's lettuce and landcress, with Winter Density the hardiest cos variety sometimes still available from the earlier sowings that have survived from the batch for autumn eating. Raw cabbage is the quickest winter salad, because you can clear one of the white domes that are savoys or January Kings, cut through the stem and get back into the warm with perhaps 3 pounds (1.3 kg) of nutritional value, that soars in shop price in hard weather.

Those who have allergies will see that there is still a wide range of the numbers that abbreviate the natural orders that they can eat each day, and also at what date they could have sown to have had them ready for eating in this dead centre month before the gardener's year starts turning again.

The leaf beets, chard and spinach beet, winter spinach and a full range of the cabbage family are ready to gather when weather permits, and the large leaves of chard can be twisted (not cut) off far more quickly than picking spinach. Never strip a single plant but take leaves in turn so that there are enough to protect the new leaves that will be ready later. It pays to pack the garden with every possible winter vegetable, to allow for losses and to give recovery time from crops that produce well into the spring. The value of wide spacing shows in winter, for leaf vegetables in contact with each other provide more shelter for slugs and hold moisture that leads to rotting.

January is seed catalogue time, and though seed potatoes and all bush or tree fruit should have been ordered early in the autumn to give a choice of varieties, it pays to place one sizeable seed order with a good firm, to secure the essentials and save on postage – there is always a surcharge on small orders, which makes afterthoughts expensive. The following varieties are likely to be available for several years to come, and are kinds with flavour of real garden merit. They may well be replaced by better varieties in the future, but it is also possible that their successors will be vegetable equivalents to tasteless Golden Delicious apples, and certain that they will be more expensive.

Vegetables of value

Broad beans
Aquadulce Claudia: the best for November sowing to dodge blackfly. A very hardy, long-pod variety.
Giant Green Windsor: four large seeds to a pod. Sow from February to April. Good Windsor flavour and fine freezer.
Hylon: a new, heavy-cropping long pod, with 10-11 seeds a pod, for autumn or spring sowing. Holds its flavour well frozen.
The Sutton: a foot high (30 cm) to sow a foot (30 cm) apart each way for succession from March to July.

Table 11: VEGETABLES FOR JANUARY EATING

Available for eating	Family	Sowing	Planting
Artichokes, Jerusalem	3	—	February-March
Beans (dried or frozen)	7	May-June	—
Beetroot (leaf)	2	April	—
Beetroot (stored)	2	May	—
Broccoli (heading)	4	May	July
Brussels sprouts	4	May	June-July
Cabbage	4	June	July
Carrots (stored)	12	May	—
Celeriac	12	March	May
Celery	12	March-April	May-June
Hamburg parsley	12	March-April	—
Kale	4	April	June-July
Lamb's lettuce	13	July-August	—
Landcress	4	August-September	—
Leeks	8	April	July
Lettuce	3	March-July	—
Miner's lettuce	10	July-August	—
Onions (stored)	8	March	—
Parsnips	12	February-March	—
Peas (dried or frozen)	7	January-May	—
Potatoes (stored)	11	—	April-May
Pumpkins	5	April	May
Radish, Chinese	4	July	—
Salsify	3	March-April	—
Scorzonera	3	March-April	—
Spinach (winter)	2	September	—
Swedes (stored)	4	July	—
Sweetcorn (frozen)	6	April-May	—
Tomatoes (bottled)	11	—	May-June
Turnips (stored)	4	June-July	—

French beans

The Prince: long pods, tender picked young and keeps going longest if continuously picked. Fewer plants supply all your beans.

Sprite: completely stringless. Continental flavour and a good freezer.

Masterpiece Stringless: long pods, early and fine flavour. Good freezer.

Runner beans

Enorma: a big bean, 21-inch (53 cm) pods, fine flavour and a good freezer.

White Achievement: rather smaller pods, but excellent dried as a butterbean or frozen.

The Czar: the finest flavoured white-seeded runner to dry as a butterbean. Introduced by Messrs Laxton in 1883 who named it for Alexander III, whose Coronation celebrations went on for a week and hit British headlines. Saved by the HDRA from the EEC in 1988.

Beetroot

Boltardy: slow to bolt from early sow-

ings.
Detroit Little Ball: a fast round beetroot for summer sowings and stores
very well.
Dobbies Purple: formerly Dell's purple,
a dark red beetroot grown for flavour
ever since 1885.

Broccoli
Purple Sprouting: to eat from March to
May, there are early and late forms;
experiment to find the best succession
in your district.

Brussels sprouts
Noisette: the longest-cropping variety,
in production from October to February. Survives hard winters.

Cabbage
April: one of the best spring cabbages.
Emerald Cross: a fast summer cabbage
excellent shredded in salads.
Red Drumhead: the only red cabbage
the EEC regulations allow, adds colour
and flavour to winter salads. Too good
to pickle. Cook it and enjoy it.
Winningstadt: a fine old autumn cab-
bage to eat from August to November.
January King: for December to March.
Ormskirk: Savoy, crinkly-leaf type, to
eat from Christmas right on into spring.
Stands hard winters.

Carrots
Early Nantes: a fast, stump-rooted kind
for spring and summer sowings.
Chantenay Red Cored: heavy yielding
maincrop that stores well.
Autumn King: the best all-round carrot. Sow in spring for summer eating,
late May or June for winter. Hardy to
lift as required in the open.

Cauliflowers
All the Year Round: a large, white,
curded variety which can be sown to be
ready at any time of year in the south.
Walcheren Winter (formerly a brocco-

li): comes through hard winters and is
ready in April.

Celeriac
Tellus: a much improved variety of the
old species.

Celery
Golden Self-Blanching: to eat from August till frost.
Solid White: needs blanching, ready
from October to January.

Cucumbers
Burpless Tasty Green: a cucumber to
grow outdoors, not of greenhouse quality. Resists mildew.

Kale
Tall Green Curled: the last survivor of
the Scots kales. Very hardy. Vitamins C
and A to go with haggis and porridge.
Thousand Head: the hardiest plain-
leaved variety. Young shoots to eat in
spring, and the most productive winter
poultry greenfood.

Kohlrabi
White Vienna: sow for succession and
eat small, raw or cooked.

Leeks
Musselburgh: a good, all-round, very
hardy leek that lasts until April.

Lettuce
Fortune: a quick-growing cabbage kind
to sow for succession up to July.
Avondefiance: for July/August sowing,
resists mildew and root aphids.
Avoncrisp: for earlier sowing. Also mildew and aphid resisting.
Windermere: the finest 'frilly' lettuce,
quick to mature and slowest to bolt,
lasting a month from a single sowing.
Large and stout midribs – a good one
weighs 1 pound (455 g), (no good com-
mercially, for lettuces are not sold by
weight, but excellent for gardeners).

Little Gem: a quick-growing, compact cos lettuce with a fine flavour. Sow March to mid-July.

Winter Density: sow in August as the hardiest winter-cos variety.

Imperial Winter: sow in September to heart in the spring. The hardiest winter cabbage kind.

Onions

Bedfordshire Champion: a long-keeping, heavy-cropping, mild variety. Buy Red Italian for a real, strong onion taste. Still legal in Italy, so buy it on holiday in Europe.

Express Yellow: the best of the Japanese varieties to sow in August and eat as early as July, ripening off faster than sets, to dry and keep.

Oakey: a large, flat onion with a strong taste, introduced in 1880 to go with cheese and realer than real Real Ale. A good cropper and keeps well.

Sturon: a round, long-keeping variety also available as sets (small bulbs) for early spring planting.

White Lisbon: the traditional spring onion to sow from March to September. Plants from early sowings, can be transplanted to grow onions for cooking quickly, if those stored have failed to keep.

Parsley

Champion Moss Curled: a closely curled kind and the hardiest, needing no protection in hard northern winters.

Parsnip

White Gem: good flavour and shorter roots than Tender and True and the show varieties, so easier to lift for storing. Resistant to canker.

Peas

Early Onward: a heavy cropper to sow in succession from March to June. Two-feet (60 cm) high so needs only low support. Freezes well.

Kelvedon Wonder: early but excellent for June-July sowings because it resists the mildew common in late cropping peas. Eighteen inches (45 cm).

Greenshaft: early main crop. Extra sweet for raw eating. Freezes well. Resists pea wilt disease. Two feet 6 inches (75 cm) when fully grown.

Pilot: the best drying pea, sown in February or March. Tall (3½ feet or 1 metre high), with a heavy crop to leave on and dry, as well as eating early as a normal pea.

Radishes

Cherry Belle: the radish that lasts longest from a single sowing without growing hot and woody.

Black Spanish Round or Long: white radish-flavoured flesh, black skin, for cooking or raw eating in winter.

China Rose: looks like a giant French breakfast radish, red and white. Both excellent grated in winter salads.

Salsify

Giant: can be lifted and stored or stay in the ground. Young shoots in the spring like asparagus.

Scorzonera

Russian Giant: black-skinned. A different flavour and rather easier to peel. Just as hardy as salsify.

Sweetcorn

First of All: the fastest finisher for the British climate; produces a freezerful, even in the north.

Tomatoes

Harbinger: won the John Innes Trial for the outdoor variety with the most ripe before 6 September in 1942. First-class flavour, thin skin and the best of all to ripen off the plant.

Turnips

Snowball: a fast, white variety to reach

eating size in about six weeks. Leave them in longer at wider spacing to delight your pony.

Golden Ball: a yellow-fleshed kind also for quick growing, and a contrasting colour grated on the salad. Good keeper.

Species, like miner's lettuce (*Claytonia perfoliata*) and herbs, are not in peril in the EEC so are not on this list of varieties worth saving on their merits. A revival of interest, especially in the older varieties, could well keep them in the catalogues indefinitely.

Think ahead to summer

January is the time to think ahead to the summer, and do every job that can be done to give more time in the headlong rush of March and April. Start saving the smaller sizes of tins, or collect from neighbours if you do not use any, taking the bottoms out with a rotary tin opener, soaking the paper off and giving them a coat inside and out of black bitumen paint, ready to place over your carrots after thinning. The carrot fly (*Psila rosea*) comes in low like a cruise missile to lay its eggs close to where the leaves start from the ground and the tin can baffle it. This is one of the many counter-measures used by organic gardeners against this pest, but it is, like all the others, not 100 per cent successful, and the inorganic answers are not much better. The tin trick is very successful against surface caterpillars or cutworms, which are the larvae of the heart and dart moth, the turnip moth, the diamond black moth and the yellow underwing, which will clear a bed of newly planted cabbages in a night.

If you find seedlings vanishing overnight from the attacks of these nocturnal caterpillars, and you have the tins already painted, you can slip them on and beat the pests. The reason for painting is firstly to stop the tins rusting and keep them smooth to provide no grip for climbing caterpillars and secondly because the black surface absorbs the heat and warms the young carrots ahead, as well as keeping the wind off them.

Compost cabbages and their pests

An even more useful pest-control measure against the mealy cabbage aphid (*Brevicoryne brassicae*) and the cabbage white fly (*Aleyrodes proletella*) can begin now. Stretch the garden line where you will be sowing the first runner beans in May and take out a trench 8 inches (20 cm) wide and deep for the first row. As your cabbages, Brussels sprouts and broccoli finish, *dig* – do not pull – the stumps up and spread them along the bottom of the trench to make a loose layer about 4 inches (10 cm) thick. Empty your daily kitchen waste on top of them, which is far better than adding them to the dormant compost heap in winter where they can attract rats. Cover each bucketful with soil at once, so the birds do not steal the waste or strew it round the garden, and tread it down, filling up the trench completely before digging the one for the next row beside it. If you dig several trenches at once the sides crumble as you stumble about with the full bucket. If any stumps show clubroot, chop the root off and dump it in the dustbin, for stems do not carry spores.

As the kitchen waste decays between the stumps, the soil will sink and need topping up before the beans are sown or planted; then as the stumps themselves rot the soil will sink further, leaving a shallow trough to fill with the hose when the beans are tall and thirsty, for the shock of cold mains water on the foliage may mean dropped blossoms. When the crop is cleared, the stumps will have decayed to lasting black humus, for you have made long, narrow compost heaps, activated by the surplus

Smashed cabbage stumps
and Brussels sprout stems

BEAN TRENCH

nitrogen fixed by the bacteria in the bean roots.

The extra value of this trick lies in killing the over-wintering eggs of two increasing pests of the cabbage family – mealy cabbage aphid (*Brevicoryne brassicae*) and cabbage white fly (*Aleyrodes proletella*), which looks like the tomato species (*Trialeurodes vaporariorum*), and attacks many greenhouse crops, especially fuchsias. It is also a tiny white moth with immobile, scale insect-like larvae, but, unfortunately, it has no parasitic wasp as an easy way to controlling it. It is helped by those who leave their Brussels sprouts in to grow 'spring greens' on the tops, and let their sprouting broccoli flower. If all growing cabbage tribe stumps or plants were either underground or burned by mid April before the first winged generation are hatched and flying, we could exterminate both pests without any sprays – organic or inorganic.

Kitchen waste alone can be used for pea trenches, especially for Pilot, the drying pea, for their bacteria do not seem vigorous enough to deal with Brussels-sprout stems. Those who do not have a 'poultry bucket' for potato peelings would do well to exclude these because they can grow from only the eyes in the peel and potatoes among the peas are weeds that should be taken out before they swamp the row.

Feed birds with your pests
If January is dry and mild enough to allow digging, turn over the ground where you had carrots, onions or cabbages, unless this is under green manure, to give the robins a chance to peck up the chrysalids of the cabbage, carrot and onion flies, and between the raspberry canes to give them another go at the pupae of the raspberry beetle (*Byturus tormentosus*). Robins' eyes can pick out pest pupae which we cannot tell from tiny stones, and this is why they follow us round the garden whenever we are digging. Almost every garden is the territory of a pair of

Attract the blue tits and get rid of aphids

robins, and it is possible to feed these useful birds rather than the starlings, by getting your local birds used to taking food from your hand. Wild bird food must be paid for, but fat is free from your butcher. Do grate some for your local robins to help them through hard winters.

The tit family – blue, great and coal – are even more easily fed and enlisted as winter helpers. Obtain a piece of fat about 4 inches (10 cm) square from your butcher, who will hopefully give it free, and hang it from the tip of a 6 foot (1.8 m) bamboo cane thrust slantwise into the rose bed. It should hang about 1 foot (30 cm) above the bushes. There will be room for at most two tits on the fat, and when food is scarce there may be as many as ten others waiting for their turns to perch and peck. These will fill in time by searching the gnarled bark round the bases of the bushes for the eggs of greenfly, so there will be none to hatch next summer and no need to spray.

Ornithologists confirm that fat is better than peanuts in nylon nets, or wild bird food for insectivorous species, because these both contain protein and are better balanced foods and so encourage the birds to rely on them. Fat is nearly pure hydrocarbons which will provide energy for small blue tits in a cold white world, but it will not encourage them to neglect their pest-eating duties. They will also hunt for protein to balance their diets and experiments at research stations where apple trees were covered with giant meat-safes to exclude all birds, showed conclusively just how many hundreds of assorted pest eggs and hibernating caterpillars tits eat.

Thin, narrow strips of fat are best and those with neglected orchards or trees too large for easy spraying, can use steps to hang fat sparingly among the branches. You are not out to feed birds quickly. It is the length of the queue that interests the gardener – because the tits, waiting like patients in the Doctor's waiting room, eat the pests. Hang fat also on ornamental cherry trees because these harbour the cherry blackfly (*Myzus cerasi*) which resists ladybirds as in neglected orchards with trees too large to prune.

The 'tit-fat trick' – perhaps the best organic gardening hint I ever found – also helps the vegetable gardener. The blackfly of broad beans (*Aphis fabae*) which also attacks French and runners, dahlias, rhubarb and nasturtiums, spends the winter on the Spindlewood

Fat attracts blue tits to eat blackfly on ornamental cherries

peaches and plums are all not for pruning, because the spores of several fungi causing the condition known as 'dieback' are blowing about. Wait till May when this risk will be over. Even apples and pears, traditionaly winter-pruned, are better done in February, to dodge *Sclerotina*, the fungus responsible for brown storage rot, which keeps commercial growers spraying from July until picking time. It is no more work to prune a little later and costs nothing.

Look carefully round the orchard in January to see if there are any fruits still hanging on, withered and lonely. They can hold the spores of a number of fungi that are better taken off with a long-arm pruner, or picked from steps, and brought in to burn on a cheerful fire than leaving them releasing millions of microscopic troublemakers next spring. If a cherry still has any leaves hanging on in January, pick them and burn them too, because this shows cherry-leaf scorch fungus (*Gnomonia erythrostoma*) with spores waiting to infect the opening leaf buds. On small trees, picking off is possible, but larger ones need spraying.

The best all-round fungicide for organic gardeners is burgundy mixture,

(*Euonymus europaeus*) and the wayfaring tree (*Viburnum lantana*) in hedges. Farmers have destroyed so many hedges that increasingly *Aphis fabae* has to hibernate on the cultivated *Viburnums* in our gardens, the many species of *Philadelphus* and especially *Euonymus* hedges, which can supply a whole suburb with an annual starting stock of blackfly. So hang up the fat freely, in December, January and February, as a hard weather bird helper only, to make sure the birds are well away before the flower buds swell, soften and grow tasty.

Fruit care in January

The first fruit problem of the year is to remember *not* to use the new secateurs you have been given for Christmas to prune stone fruit. Apricots, cherries, damsons, greengages, nectarines,

Take the trouble to pick off mummified fruit as they hold pest eggs and disease spores

for its copper does no harm to anything other than fungi (unlike lime-sulphur which harms many varieties known as 'sulphur-shy' and kills useful predators such as *Anthocoris nemorum* and its relatives) and it reaches the ground in trace-element quantities. It can be bought ready made-up, but if copper sulphate can be obtained, dissolve 8 ounces in 1 gallon (225 g in 4.5 l) of boiling water and 1 pound of washing soda in a gallon (455 g in 4.5 l) of cold. Mix the two with a further three gallons (13.6 l) of cold water in a plastic container, because the copper can react with metal. Spray this mixture on in December and January, when the buds are at their most dormant, and nothing but fungi will be harmed. In addition to cherry-leaf scorch, it is the best answer to peach-leaf curl (*Taphrina deformans*) and the less common cherry-leaf curl (*T. minor*), and is also quite effective against apple scab (*Venturia inaequalis*). A cheaper and easier remedy for this one is urine sprayed neat on the branches, for the 2.3 per cent of urea it contains is just as effective from every gardener's private supply as the synthetic chemical sold in bulk to commercial fruit growers.

January is the month to destroy the plum-curl aphid (*Brachycaudus helichrysi*), which is extremely difficult to kill at its summer stage inside the curled leaves, but easy if you catch it when it has just hatched in January and Febru-

ary and is creeping into the bud scales, and before it starts to multiply like microchips. The paraffin emulsion used in the past can be made with soap flakes. Dissolve 4 ounces (115 g) of these in 1 pint (0.5 l) of hot water, and add to this 16 fluid ounces (.454 l) of ordinary paraffin. Stir this up rapidly with enough extra water (cold) to make 1 gallon (4.5 l) and spray it on. This is also effective against the hibernating stage of American blight or woolly aphid (*Eriosoma lanigerum*) which is *not* repelled by nasturtiums trained up the trees – by the time these flower the creature has gone into hiding. Spraying with paraffin emulsion at the right time will hit it hard.

One of the last January jobs among the fruit is to take off the suckers which spring up round so many trees, especially if they are grafted on the old Mussel stock for stone fruit and ornamental trees of the same family, which can come up all over the lawn. Dig away the soil round the tree until you can grip the sucker shoot firmly and *twist* it off as though you were unscrewing it. This tears out the 'heel' from which it springs and once this is destroyed there will be no more trouble. Where suckers have been cut again and again with secateurs and made a large mass, it is worth taking a large adjustable spanner as though you were a mechanic rather than a gardener, and 'unscrewing' the sucker base to burn, because these are favourite hiding places for many pests.

CHAPTER 5
FEBRUARY

The celery will be finished, but otherwise the available foods are the same as in January though the pumpkins may well give out before the end of the month. It is rarely that pumpkins can be kept after Christmas, because they miss the long, hot autumns of the USA and other warmer places which toughen and seal their skins. Inspect them as they hang, in the nylon net bags greengrocers have free for the asking, from the rafters in the attic with the onions. They may well have soft spots which show decay and should be sawn open and the firm orange flesh salvaged and cooked for deep freezing in serving-sized bags for soups and cooking as a vegetable. It is worth the deep freezer space, unlike the marrow. Never hang pumpkins up by their stalks – these tear away, leaving a wound that starts decay.

Pumpkins cannot compare with potatoes for concentrated food value (see Table 12), but the Japanese varieties are worth finding. As the seed keeps ten years it is worth buying plenty, for only a few are sown each season. Save the largest and fattest seeds from the most mature stored specimens in the attic.

Start sprouting seed potatoes
The seed potatoes should have arrived by now and begin their twelve-week stay in the 'chitting trays'. These should be the non-returnable wood trays with raised corners that hold imported grapes and tomatoes and are worth paying for because they last several seasons. Set the seed tubers 'rose end' (the end with the eyes in) upwards, and stack the trays – one on top of the other if you have to save space – in a frost-free shed, under a greenhouse staging or in a spare bedroom, for they need light and a temperature of 8-10°C.

The ideal seed potato is the size of the smallest grade of hen's egg, but today the growers expect to sell their whole crop at seed price, instead of taking the eating potato rate for the large ones. Tubers bigger than 'large'-egg size are best cut. Slice them from the rose end down, leaving three good eyes on each half, and dip the cut surface in garden lime to dry it and prevent decay. Set the cut tubers in the trays, with the cut surfaces away from each other, and inspect them at intervals to remove any that have decayed. So long as the sprouts are sturdy, potatoes lose nothing by waiting in the chitting trays for even sixteen weeks, in savage springs, or waiting for a winter crop to finish.

Though the variety of potatoes sold by greengrocers must now be written on the bag, the wholesaler will have treated them with an anti-sprouting chemical, so they cannot be a source of cheap seed. Organically grown potatoes will not have had any chemical treatment, and can be safely bought and put straight in the chitting trays in February.

Today there is less and less choice of potatoes, now that the most famous British seedsman stocks only two varieties. There is a constant procession of new varieties from the plant-breeding centres, with greater yields,

Table 12: VEGETABLES FOR FEBRUARY EATING

Available for eating	Family	Sowing	Planting
Artichokes, Jerusalem	3	—	February-March
Beans (dried or frozen)	7	May-June	—
Beetroof (leaf)	2	April	—
Beetroot (stored)	2	May	—
Broccoli (heading)	4	May	July
Brussels sprouts	4	May	June-July
Cabbage	4	June	July
Carrots (stored)	12	May	—
Celeriac	12	March	May
Hamburg parsley	12	March-April	—
Kale	4	April	June-July
Lamb's lettuce	13	July-August	—
Landcress	4	August-September	—
Leeks	8	April	July
Lettuce	3	March-July	—
Miner's lettuce	10	July-August	—
Onions (stored)	8	March	—
Parsnips	12	February-March	—
Peas (dried or frozen)	7	January-May	—
Potatoes (stored)	11	—	April-May
Pumpkins	5	April	May
Radish, Chinese	4	July	—
Salsify	3	March-April	—
Scorzonera	3	March-April	—
Spinach (winter)	2	September	—
Swedes (stored)	4	July	—
Sweetcorn (frozen)	6	April-May	—
Tomatoes (bottled)	11	—	May-June
Turnips (stored)	4	June-July	—

Table 13: COMPARATIVE FOOD VALUES OF POTATO, PUMPKIN AND MARROW

	Potato (boiled) (per cent)	Japanese pumpkin (per cent)	American pumpkin (per cent)	Marrow (per cent)
Moisture	76.40	86.90	97.2	97.8
Carbohydrate	19.70	8.10	1.40	1.40
Protein	2.10	1.80	0.50	0.40
Calcium	1-1	0.04	0.03	1-1
Phosphorus	1-1	0.04	0.01	1-1
Carotene mg per kilogram	1-1	27.00	5.90	1-1

resistance to diseases and qualities like high dry matter. Flavour, however, is a question of taste. The following varieties are all available today and at least some will be stocked by garden centres for the next few years.

Potato varieties

First earlies

Arran Pilot: heavy early cropper, some scab resistance.

Duke of York: not so fast. Fine flavour, yellow flesh and will keep until April left in to grow large. Dig the first for scraping new, and eat the last baked in their jackets.

Epicure: heavy early cropper. Deep eyes. Fine flavour, recovers best from destruction of shoots by late frosts, so good in the north.

Home Guard: high yield. High dry matter, some scab resistance. Picks up any taint from soil, especially BHC. Safe grown organically.

Sharpes Express: high dry matter, very fine flavour, lower yield early. Will keep left in to grow large.

Ulster Sceptre: high yield early. Best drought resister.

Second earlies

Maris Peer: resists scab, high dry matter. Some blight resistance.

Wilja: high yielder. Some blight resistance.

Maincrops

Arran Consul: the potato that grows old gracefully. Late sprouting. Good cooker.

Desirée: pink skinned. Good flavour and cooking quality, the most popular maincrop today, beating King Edward. Resists drought but the most subject to scab. Good keeper.

Kerr's Pink: has the thickest foliage for weed suppression, and is a chip-shop favourite, because the chips do not dis-

colour without water.

Maris Piper: fine flavour. Resists *Globodera rostochiensis*, one potato eelworm, but not *G. pallida*, the other one. A good maincrop.

Record: the finest flavour maincrop. High dry matter.

Plant artichokes now

Globe artichokes are like asparagus – not worth the trouble in small gardens for the food produced from their space, but the Jerusalem artichoke, with its knobby, cream-coloured tubers, is easy, hardy and very welcome to anyone allergic to potatoes. The best variety is Fuseau, which is the least knobby, and a tapered shape, which is scarce. Artichokes have no disease or viruses and greengrocers are the best source of supply. Once you find Fuseau or a less-knobby strain of the common type, you can keep it going indefinitely.

Start the bed by digging in a barrow-load of manure or compost to 4 square yards (3.3 m²), and plant your tubers in 6 inch (15 cm) deep trowel holes, 18 inches (45 cm) apart and 3 feet (1 m) between rows. Keep down the weeds by hoeing and as they grow tall like sunflowers, they will need stakes at the ends and middle of the rows so that strings can be run each side of them in windy gardens. Once the plants are over a foot high they need no more hoeing and can be lifted as required from November onwards, leaving enough to replant the bed next February or March.

The only pest of artichokes is a small, grey, root aphid which will be found hiding on the tubers at lifting time. The answer is to move the bed and wash the tubers in the cheapest powerful insecticide before replanting. Simmer ¾ pound (350 g) of filter-tip cigarette ends in 1 gallon (4.5 l) of water for half an hour – these are about 0.1 per cent nicotine and a serious risk to the health of pests, from aphids to caterpillars.

Strain the clear, brown liquid through nylon tights, and use it neat for caterpillars or diluted with a further gallon of water for aphids. Non-smokers can obtain cigarette ends from pubs, cinemas and bingo halls, storing their stock in a large tin, for nicotine is a deadly poison, but no one will mistake your hoarded ends for sweets. Boil it up as required, keep it off your skin and treat it with caution. Nicotine is used by organic gardeners because it spares ladybirds and their larvae, and breaks down in forty-eight hours. The cigarette-end concoction costs nothing, so can be used freely when required. It is now illegal to sell, nicotine but there is as yet no law against cigarette ends, and the deadlier paraquat is still on sale.

The dried stems of artichokes can be cut for light staking, or even compost in November, but you cannot cut down the growing stems for compost without harming the crop of tubers which should be about the same as early potatoes from the same area, far better from tubers lifted and replanted each year than left to crowd in a neglected bed. The analysis is very like that of a potato but they hold about seven times as much calcium. This is excellent for those on a milk-free diet, because there is no oxalic acid to lock it up.

Try and get your family accustomed to eating new vegetables – artichokes are so easy and nutritious that it is worth learning to like their rather smoky taste. It is unfortunate for children whose parents proclaim, 'Of course all they *really* like is frozen peas, chips, fish fingers and ice-cream', because they will grow up to be just customers, rather than experimenting gardeners who enjoy a wide range of foods.

Remember rhubarb

February is also rhubarb-planting time, and after fifteen years or more the familiar nameless shapes at the bottom of the garden show rotten hollows in the black surface stems which are signs of wear. Select the strongest with fat pink buds at the ends and cut them off with about 9 inches (23 cm) of thick stem without rotten hollows. There is no need to rotate rhubarb, but if you can spare another space for a permanent planting, you can remove your offsets or crowns for the new bed, and leave the old in production until its successor can take over. Newly planted crowns must have a year without picking to get established.

Scatter 2 pounds (1 kg) of bonemeal to the square yard (0.83 m^2) on the new bed, then dig it over with care to remove perennial weed roots, tucking a barrow-load of compost or well-rotted manure to 2 square yards (1.7 m^2) well down in the trench bottoms. Then plant your crown upright with the bud just peeping through the surface, 2 feet (60 cm) apart and 3 feet (1 metre) between rows. There is room to grow two staggered rows of lettuces between each two of rhubarb the first summer.

The best variety is Glaskin's Perpetual, which is the lowest in oxalic acid so it can be eaten even in August, but never strip a crown, because even rhubarb needs its rest and the leaves are gathering energy to feed the roots for next spring's forcing, for it is the easiest and most welcome first fruit in every garden. Early Victoria and Timperley Early are both excellent flavour kinds.

Existing beds should have been covered thickly with leafmould in November, and they are now ready to force. Once this was done under bottomless buckets or brown tin-baths, but even rhubarb must enter the plastic age, for the large earthenware drainpipes that also served are now scarce and costly. Find plastic containers, not necessarily buckets, such as the drums in which many industrial products are delivered. They should be large enough to fit over a thriving crown, about 12-15 inches (30-45 cm) across the open top, and about the same height or taller. Melt a hole in the bottom about 2 inches (5 cm) in diameter over a candle flame to provide light for the shoots to draw towards, and coat the outside of the container with black bitumen paint. Plastic is not sufficiently opaque to drive the shoots towards the light, and the dark surface will concentrate the spring sunlight, to give you solar-heated rhubarb rather more quickly than from the bottomless buckets of the past.

Sowings for February

The 500-gauge polythene sheet used to cover manure heaps is also of value in gaining growing time in spring. Dig over the beds where onions, carrots, lettuces, parsnips and early peas will be sown in March, and cover these with the useful polythene weighed down with bricks or long, heavy wood, to warm up and escape the rain. It is always a question of whether it is better to wait till the soil has warmed and the tide of spring is flowing, or to go ahead and get the work done before the rush, risking cold drying winds and savage mice and birds.

Parsnips can be sown towards the end of February, and this early sowing is worth it for those who eat small roots as early as August. The main crop for storing should wait till the second week in April because later sowings lower the canker risk and store better. Start the bed with 1 pound (455 g) of lime and 8 ounces (225 g) fish or meat and bonemeal to 4 square yards (3.3 m²) unless the soil had compost the previous year, fork it lightly in and rake level before sowing the seed in clusters of four at 9 inch (23 cm) intervals along 1 inch-deep (2.5 cm) furrows a foot (30 cm) apart. Because the parsnips will take about twenty days to show and this is time for them to be swamped by weeds, sow radishes in the gaps between the clusters before closing the furrows with the hoe blade.

The radishes will be up fast to pull as the first new salad crop of the season, and when it is clear which is the best in each bunch of parsnips, the others can be pulled out to give it room. Beyond hoeing to keep the weeds down the parsnips need little further attention. They may be attacked by celery-leaf miner, which tunnels the leaves in pale-green, wandering streaks. Spray with nicotine, which gets through the thin skin of the leaf, or, if only a few leaves suffer, pick them off. Do not grow lovage in your herb bed because this perennial vegetable harbours the celery-leaf miner through the winter and can start an attack earlier than the usual August.

Another crop that gains from an early start is onions from sets. Prepare the ground as for the parsnips – in fact they can well go next to them on the root bed – but go over their ground, treading it firm, raking level and then rolling it, because onions must have firm soil to push against when they heave themselves out to sit on the surface and ripen in the sun. Even on a heavy clay, if the soil has been dried out under plastic, it will not puddle provided it has had lime and humus. Plant the near pea-sized bulblets 6 inches (15 cm) apart and 1 foot (30 cm) between rows, using a dibber, twisting off the dry tops so that nothing shows when the soil is firmed back with the dibber point. If the dry top shows the sparrows will assume it is good nesting material and uproot all the sets.

Garlic is not so much a vegetable or a herb as a way of life. Many authorities consider that the valuable medicinal and nutritional qualities for which it is famous are present only in organically grown cloves. It is possible to buy greengrocer's garlic bulbs, split these into cloves and plant them, but this will mean a late crop that may not ripen well, because it will be a variety selected for Italy or the south of France. Buy a planting variety (ideally organically grown) in January and get them split and planted in full sun before February ends, preparing the ground and spacing as you would for onion sets. Keep them hoed through the summer and lift them when the foliage is yellow (about August) to hang in bunches in the sun, taking them under cover at night before dewfall in the evening. The drier they are the better they keep.

The first peas can go in during February and are best tipped into a basin and swirled with paraffin as a bird and mouse discourager. If there are no trenches ready with winter kitchen waste, take out a 6 inch (15 cm) deep trench and tread the partly rotted top of a compost heap into the bottom 3 inches (8 cm) then fill up with soil. Sow the peas 2 inches (5 cm) apart in two rows with 3 inches (8 cm) between them, covered with about 1 inch (2.5 cm) of soil.

Wire pea-guards should be bent over the rows and blocked at the ends. This not only keeps the birds off, but makes it safe to set mousetraps in the row so you can catch field mice without harming your robins. Peas appreciate the hollow made as the compost or refuse sinks to hold water, for in dry years each sowing lasts longer if it is given generous hosings.

The pea rows can be 30 inches (75 cm) apart, which leaves room to make the first and most useful sowing of a summer spinach such as Nobel or Jovita, down the middle of the space between the rows in a ½ inch deep (13 mm) furrow. Thin to 6 inches (15 cm) apart and eat the thinnings, then pick the leaves hard for salads, for at this time of year they are low in oxalic acid, as rhubarb is, and up to 79 mg calcium per 100 grams, which is three times more than they contain cooked.

Countering clubroot

Summer cabbage and summer cauliflower are both worth sowing in February, under pea guards because of the bird risk to the young plants; sow them in the cabbage-tribe section of the rotation and aim to keep these two to the minimum. Clubroot is most active in summer, and if lettuces can provide your summer green vegetables rather than cabbages, the lower your clubroot level will be.

The latest recommendation from the National Vegetable Research Station against clubroot is to give a really heavy dressing of lime, 2 pounds per square yard (900 g per 0.83 m^2) to the cabbage section of the rotation, dig it in, and then sow your plants. If this is done repeatedly there is a risk that too much lime will lock up the boron in the soil. This causes crown canker in beetroot, with the centre leaves dying and the roots rotting from the outside; brown patches on cauliflower curds; brown hearts in turnips and tomato fruit, with uneven ripening and brown corky spots. The answer is to dissolve 1 ounce (25 g) of borax (which is a mixture of

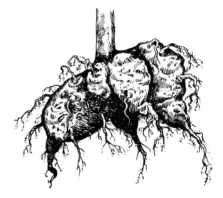

Dig, do not pull, cabbage stumps. If the rotten mass that the roots become breaks off in the soil the tiny spores last up to 20 years.

salts of boron and sodium, used for gargling and which makes an excellent ant poison mixed thoroughly with equal parts of icing sugar and left under cover where ants will find it) in 2 gallons (9 l) of hot water and water it on over 10 square yards (8.3 m^2). These problems, especially fruit spot in tomatoes, have happened in very chalky gardens, but a little too much borax would be a minor problem compared with the value of conquering clubroot.

Fruit in February

The winter pruning of apples consists of shortening the leaders, which are the longest and strongest shoots that grew last summer on every branch, by a third of their length. Then snip off their lesser contemporaries after the third, fourth or fifth bud – whichever points away from the centre of the tree. If the tree is a tip bearer, carrying its fruit on the ends of the branches like Worcester

Destroy the egg bracelets of the lackey moth as you prune your apples

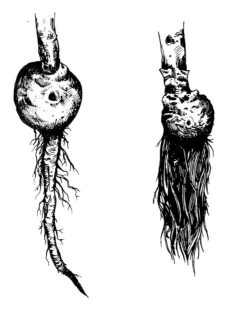

If the 'clubs' of the suspected clubroot victim are ball-shaped, cut one open. It may have a turnip gall weevil maggot inside and not be clubroot at all

Pearmain, Blenheim Orange or Irish Peach, all it will need is to have the weakest branch or two sawn out each year together with any that are crossing, crowding or have dead wood on them.

The late Charles Hapgood, the best organic fruit grower in Britain once said, 'The most important part of any successful orchard is a man with a good lens who knows what he is looking for.' Searching the bare branches in February gives the best opportunity to prune away problems and one of these is the lackey moth (*Malacasoma neustria*), which produces hairy caterpillars up to an inch and a half long (4 cm), that are blue-grey with red and white stripes, devouring leaves and shoots. They spin web nests on branch forks or knit together leaves in which they hide from sprays and their natural enemy – the cuckoo, which is out early in orchards to hear the munching of the first caterpillar. The lackey moth overwinters as eggs laid in the autumn, in bands of 100-200 that almost look like tiny table napkin rings. Destroy them with your secateurs, for they resist even powerful inorganic winter washes. If the moths suddenly arrive, you have a problem. The organic answer is to keep your eyes open and take action at the right time, before they hatch in April. Check cotoneasters, eucryphias, hawthorns, especially the lovely double-flowered standards, lilacs, roses and pyracanthas for the distinctive eggbands – they could start on these and spread to your apples.

Normal trees, like Cox's Orange Pippin and James Grieve also need any branches that are crossing or crowding the centre sawn out now, but this and ordinary pruning are less important than a thorough search for canker, which is caused by the fungus *Nectria galligena*) infecting damaged bark from the scrape of a small boy's climbing boot, a graze from a careless pruning saw, or wounds from airgun pellets fired at bullfinches, or damage from the tiny punctures in the bark made by woolly aphid.

The cankers grow like craters in the bark surrounded by rough ridges and gradually girdle a branch until this dies. When small branches and spurs are cankered, cut these right out until the wood shows white, but with large branches – especially at forks – cut away the canker, using a chisel to get into clean wood.

Saw off all dead wood for burning because this can spread the spores of *N. cinnabarina*), related to apple canker, but also causing branches to wilt and die suddenly in summer on black- and red-

Apple canker. Saw the canker out at pruning time

currants, gooseberries and a number of ornamentals. This shows as pinhead-sized pink pustules on dead wood in summer, autumn and winter, with dark red versions in spring. These can also grow and spread spores from cut branches and prunings left in orchards, and even old pea sticks. Burn all this rubbish – prevention is better and cheaper than chemical cure.

It is orthodox practice to coat pruning cuts more than an inch (2.5 cm) across with a tree paint that keeps out spores but leaves existing infection still growing. The organic answer is the 'anti-fungus fungus' (the garden equivalent to an 'anti-missile missile' in armaments terminology) *Trichoderma viride*) now sold as Binab T, a spore powder making a paste for treating all tree wounds or a spray for small cuts. The dry powder keeps three years, but once wet should be used up within four hours and not later than 48 hours after the wounds were made.

The worst infection from apple and pear scab (*Venturia inaequalis*) comes from the last spores of summer showing as small, blistered swellings at the bases of the shoots that should be shortened to spurs. Cut these out for burning and spray with Binab T as directed on the tin. As 80 per cent of the scab spores

The March moth lays smaller, slanting 'bracelets' between January and April. Look for these and destroy them

overwinter on dead leaves, either sweep them up for burning with deadwood rubbish and prunings in one of the rare bonfires organic gardeners make, or run the rotary mower over them as they lie. This is best done as soon as all have fallen, and breaks them up (if the knives are set low) into bite-sized portions for the worms to take under, enjoying the spores on the worm scale equivalent to mushrooms on toast, building humus rather than trouble for next year.

Apple scab can also be seen on the bark of year-old shoots, that is, the sections of the spurs and leaders left at last year's pruning time. The smooth young bark will be wrinkled, torn and split, and the exposed portions will be covered with black patches that produce the spores. Prune these out, taking out the small, spurred branches with a pruning saw, and, like all apple prunings, burn them and hoard the ashes as these will be high in potash.

Then spray with burgundy mixture at its dormant stage against both scab and apple mildew (*Podosphaera leucotricha*). The last is best sought at blossom time, and looks like a white powder on the unfolding buds in spring. Remove any infected spurs and burn, for they will not fruit anyway. There are many mildew spores in the ordinary wood buds, and pruning removes these; if tip bearers show mildew, shorten their shoots by about 3 inches (7 cm). Another disease to watch for when the blossom opens is blossom wilt (*Sclerotinia laxa*), when young leaves round the trusses wilt and die, followed by the blossom itself. The only answer is to prune out the attacked spurs and burn them. Infected spurs may have small grey cushions of fungus on them, so should be cut out completely. Luckily this disease is rare.

Pears are pruned in the same way as apples, and should be sprayed in February, before their earlier blossom starts, with burgundy mixture against pear scab, pear leaf blister (*Taphrina bullata*), which is related to peach leaf curl, and *Phytophthora cactorum*, which produces brown patches on the fruit. It is even more important to remove mummified fruit left on from last year because this harbours pear midge as well as *Phytophthora* spores.

The pear leaf blister mite (*Eriophyes piyi*) breeds five generations a year and in February, when it is waking up and still hibernating under the bud scales, paraffin emulsion will catch it when the leaves are just beginning to open. It is better to wait till you see green or reddish blisters on the leaves. Pick them off and burn them so you stop the first generation, for the fifth can strip the leaves off a tree.

The American gooseberry mildew (*Spaerotheca morsuvae*) is the curse of many gardens, and though the spores are tough, they are spreading in February. A remedy that has been found effective in Canada is to spray the bushes with neat urine just before the leaf buds open, and three weeks later with urine diluted with three parts of water. In Canada the neat urine spray for apple and pear scab is given just before the leaf buds open.

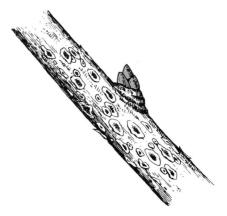

Scab spores on young shoot. Snip them off when you are pruning

CHAPTER 6
MARCH

Once it was said that March came in like a lion and went out like a lamb, and that a peck of March dust was worth half a load of hay compared with a full load for a swarm of bees in May. Today our springs are dry and cold, but it is still worth neglecting the lawn and the television to get as much sown as possible, even if there are losses and we must sow again in April. Sowing for the long-term, slow-growing, cabbage-tribe plants like sprouting broccoli and savoys can wait till April, so can beetroot because these store better small. Those whose stores are running low and who need new supplies urgently will get in a small batch in March and more later.

Vegetable sowing and growing in March

Broad beans are potash hungry and can take as much as 8 ounces (225 g) a square yard (0.83 m²) of wood ashes. This will be available more rapidly than rock potash, which should have gone on in the autumn before crops like beans, potatoes and tomatoes are planted. The Sutton, sown 1 foot (30 cm) apart each way at monthly intervals, will take over from the autumn-sown Aquadulce Claudia, with the last sowing in July. Plant with a dibber 2 inches (5 cm) deep and hoe perhaps once before their bushiness takes over. Eat the first in the pods and shell them as they get tougher, clearing each batch for compost. Only experience teaches exactly how many of everything a family needs, even if they need broad beans

right through the summer.

The Windsor and Longpod beans need more room, but produce a heavier crop. Sow them 3 inches (8 cm) deep, 8 inches (20 cm) apart along the line, then move this 6 inches (15 cm) down the garden and plant another row, spaced to come in between the others. The staggered rows hold each other up, though stakes and string at the end of rows are advisable later; if you need more than a double row, allow 30 inches (75 cm) between them for picking room.

Broad beans are easy, but the more beans the fewer peas, and both Pilot for drying, and Early Onward or Kelvedon Wonder for freezing, should be sown in March, just like the earlies in February. Remember that the drying peas are going to stay longer in their room than those picked green, and that peas eaten fresh (ideally raw in salads) are nicer than frozen. The spacing is standard, because as the peas and beans clear, they are just cut off at ground level to leave their nitrogen-rich roots in the soil ready for the cabbage-tribe crops to plant directly without digging in the firm soil.

Freezers, like fire, are good servants but bad masters and filling a freezer with frozen peas will give a poor diet compared with the crops you could have grown for fresh eating or shed storage in the same space. People with allergies, who must have a rotation of different meats, as well as meat eaters, will get the best value from fetching meat ready cut up in meal-sized packs

Table 14: VEGETABLES FOR MARCH EATING

Available for eating	Family	Sowing	Planting
Artichokes, Jerusalem	3	—	February-March
Beans (dried or frozen)	7	May-June	—
Beetroot (stored)	2	May	—
Broccoli (early sprouting)	4	April	June
Brussels sprouts	4	May	June-July
Cabbage	4	June	July
Carrots (stored)	12	May	—
Celeriac	12	March	May
Kale	4	April	June-July
Lamb's lettuce	13	July-August	—
Landcress	4	August-September	—
Leeks	8	April	July
Lettuce	3	March-July	—
Miner's lettuce	10	July-August	—
Onions (stored)	8	March	—
Peas (dried or frozen)	7	January-May	—
Potatoes (stored)	11	—	April-May
Radish, Chinese	4	July	—
Rhubarb	9	April	February
Salsify	3	March-April	—
Scorzonera	3	March-April	—
Spinach (winter)	2	September	—
Swedes (stored)	4	July	—
Sweetcorn (frozen)	6	April-May	—
Tomatoes (bottled)	11	—	May-June
Turnips (stored)	4	June-July	—

from an organic farm. Freezers are useful time savers, for baking wholemeal bread ahead and cooking for a big weekend, but if we fill them with root vegetables which would just as well keep in ashes, sand or peat, or tomatoes and bush fruit which could be bottled, we are wasting an asset. Bought frozen vegetables may have been treated with substances that give a brighter colour but lock up useful minerals so they pass wasted from our bodies, apart from the question of allergic reactions. Our own frozen foods may well be many shades less colourful than bought, but we know exactly what is in them.

If we sow a fast round beetroot like Detroit Little Ball in March we can eat it in June, and June sowings will be cricket-ball size for storing by October. The policy for those who want to eat beetroot over the longest period is to sow single rows and start eating them at golf-ball size, sowing extra rows later for storing. Sow the large seeds like tiny, dried raspberries in pairs at 6 inch (15 cm) intervals along furrows 8 inches (20 cm) apart, which leaves just enough room for hoeing. As beetroot belong to 'No. 2' they can be grown without rotation with spinach and the other vegetables marked with asterisks in Table 1, anywhere they will fit in.

Carrots, too, can be sown in two

batches – one now to take over from the shrinking hoard in store and a summer sowing for storage, which may be smaller than normal, but will dodge the worst of the carrot fly. They need a fine, sandy soil or a clay that has been given ample leafmould or compost and are best following a crop that was manured the previous year. Dry the soil out under polythene, mix the fine seed with eight times its bulk of fine bonemeal so that as little as ½ ounce (14 g) of seed fills 200 feet (60 m) of ½-inch (1 cm) deep furrows 8 inches (20 cm) apart, and the cream colour of the bonemeal shows up well against the dark soil. Early carrots should be short, fat and fast, so Early Nantes or Amsterdam Forcing are the best for these first sowings.

Salsify and scorzonera have long, large seeds and it is easy to sow them individually at 8-inch (20 cm) intervals along 1 inch-deep (2.5 cm) furrows 8 inches (20 cm) apart. They can be lifted and stored or eaten as required, but sow extra salsify because of the value of the young shoots you could be eating now. Surround the salsify bed reserved for forcing with 1 foot-high (30 cm) wire-netting (brick reinforcement netting can be bought from a builders' merchant, which costs less and lasts longer) stapled to short posts. Fill up the enclosure with leafmould when the salsify leaves have died down, and scrape it away in March when the young leaves – like wide, folded grass blades – show through the leafmould. Pick them and either chop and serve raw in salads or cook as a spinach with an asparagus flavour. The roots taste of oysters, hence the popular name of 'oyster plant', but they could equally well be called 'no-trouble asparagus' because of the value of the spring shoots. These continue in production until June, when they run up and flower with sweet sultan-like blooms about 2 inches (5 cm) across. Like scorzonera, which has yellow, daisy flowers and wide, hairy, non-edible leaves, salsify is a species and if a few flowers are allowed to ripen their dandelion-like seedheads, enough will grow to sow and give away for years. They do not cross-pollinate because, like elephants and rhinoceroses, they have different chromosomes.

Salsify foliage is too good to compost if you have chickens, because the flower stems are the green food they like best of all, perhaps because it is so rich in iron, without oxalic acid to lock it up. This stains the fingers red when you pick or prepare the shoots, but it comes off easily with *cold* water. Some people like the scorzonera roots more than those of salsify, once they learn not to peel them but to boil in the black skin which comes off more easilty when rubbed in a cloth while still hot.

Prepare the ground for onions from seed, exactly as for sets, sowing in ½-inch (1 cm) deep furrows 1 foot (30 cm) apart and thinning to 6 inches (15 cm) between plants. They need the extra space to allow room for bending the foliage over to help ripening in July or August. If the stored onions run low, transplant some of the August-sown White Lisbon spring onions that should be ready to pull for salads now to 6-inch (15 cm) each way spacing, and let them grow on to golf-ball size. They will not keep, but will fill the gap before the set grown onions are ripe. Those who have sown no spring onions can buy a bunch at a greengrocer's and plant them now. It is possible to snip the tips of the leaves off these repeatedly to add an onion taste to salads without spoiling the bulbs below – an example of eating your cake and having it, rare in gardening.

Parsley normally takes four to six weeks to germinate, and though it can be speeded up considerably by soaking it in urine overnight, it is best to sow radishes along the ½-inch (1 cm) deep furrow for the single row which is all that is needed in view of the alkaloid, despite its excellent analysis. Hamburg parsley provides parsley-flavoured foliage – lower in the alkaloid – and roots. Sow the seeds in threes, 8 inches (20 cm) apart and between rows, thinning to the best and keeping them hoed through the summer. They will be ready to dig in November and store or to leave in the ground all the winter, which gives the advantage of the foliage staying green for picking as a parsley substitute. The roots can be boiled or steamed like carrots or parsnips, which they rather resemble, or grated raw in salad. The large roots have the best flavour, so sow early on well-composted ground, with 4 ounces a square yard (115 g per 0.83 m²) of fine bonemeal or blood, fish and bone before sowing if the soil is poor.

The reason unusual vegetables stay rare is because most gardeners leave them in too long while their wives wonder how to cook the strange monsters dumped in the kitchen. Kohlrabi is an unusual but useful vegetable, which looks like a turnip out of the ground and is in fact a kind of cabbage with a swollen stem for eating. It needs to be sown for succession, perhaps every four weeks – the last in June. Sow thinly first in March in ½-inch (1 cm) deep furrows 8 inches (20 cm) apart and thin to 8 inches (20 cm) between plants, leaving the thinnings to grow about 2 inches (5 cm) tall, so they can be pulled to add their nutty flavour to salads. Ten weeks from sowing, their stem bulges should be rather smaller than cricket balls, and ready to pull, cutting the leaves off for compost, for pulling breaks the skin and loses flavour. Do not peel; merely wash and boil like turnips. They can be eaten as ordinary turnips; sliced after boiling and fried with egg and breadcrumbs, diced to

serve cold with mayonnaise, like potato salad, or grated raw. Alternatively, slice them into sticks and serve raw in glasses like a wholefood equivalent to potato crisps to eat with a clever but rather devious little home-made wine. The main value of kohlrabi lies in the high vitamin A – 2,500 IUs per 100 g, or about sixteen times as much as cabbage and twenty-five times that of cauliflower, though they are not in the carrot class. The thinnings transplant well to the same spacing for a later batch from each sowing.

The autumn-sown lettuces will be starting to heart, and the value of having plenty is that they can be cut to fill a salad bowl when they are still only leaves. March is the time for the first outdoor sowings, but if plants from seed grown under glass early in February are available, they can be bought and planted out from the middle of the month when the weather turns more lamb-like. Take what you can get, with All the Year Round an old favourite of taste, and Cheshunt Early Ball and Lobjoit's Green Cos likely purchases to be ready in May.

Fortune is the fastest cabbage-type lettuce for March sowing thinly in ½-inch (1 cm) deep furrows 8 inches (20 cm) apart, thinning to 8 inches (20 cm) between plants staggered in the rows. Windermere, the finest frilly or 'crisp heart' variety needs spacing 1 foot (30 cm) apart each way, with the same staggering, because they grow so large and last up to four weeks without bolting. Transplant some thinnings from each sowing to bring on a later batch and sow every six weeks rather than every four.

Little Gem, the tastiest of the cos varieties should be thinned to only 6 inches (15 cm) because it is smaller, though it needs 8 inches (20 cm) between the rows to allow for hoeing, rubber banding to blanch them and selection. Winter Density, the best winter cos variety can also be sown in spring and summer for those who like a larger cos, spacing 8 inches (20 cm) each way.

Miner's lettuce and lamb's lettuce, otherwise known as 'corn salad', are the two odd men out among the natural orders which provide salads almost round the year for allergy sufferers. For normal gardeners they are useful hardy winter salads, far hardier than any lettuce, and can be grown every winter through frost and snow even in the most clubroot-haunted garden.

The best of the two is miner's lettuce, *Claytonia perfoliata*, (also known as 'winter purslane') named because it is found wild from Canada to California where the miners in the 1849 gold rush (and their 'daughters Clementine' for those who remember the old song) ate it as their only green food to go with salt pork, beans and 'dampers' of flour, fat and salt. It can be eaten for nine months of the year in Britain and in 1982 it throve under the snow as a far better source of vitamin C than any expensive greenhouse lettuce. Analysed for the first time in January 1982 by the HDRA *Claytonia* showed 24 mg per 100 g compared with 3.4 for greenhouse lettuce, which is why it was so valuable in balancing a diet in which deer meat was the only fresh food.

The seeds are tiny, but keep for five years in the packet in an ordinary drawer, so there is no need to sow too thickly and 'use up the packet'. Mix the seed with about six times its bulk of fine bonemeal, which may be more expensive than fine sand but is about the same weight as small light seed, and sow it along the bottoms of ½-inch (1 cm) deep furrows the standard 8 inches (20 cm) apart. It is worth making white painted measuring sticks for the standard spacings to use with ordinary garden line. Thin the seedlings to 6 inches

Miner's lettuce, the best of the unusual winter salads

(15 cm) apart so they just meet in the rows when full sized, which, with this early sowing, will be by the end of May. In April the last of the winter crop runs to seed and there is a gap before the March sowing is ready to eat in June.

Lamb's lettuce, *Valerianella olitoria*, was a weed of cornfields in Europe when 'corn' meant wheat, oats, rye and barley, as sold by corn-chandlers, not as maize made into 'cornflakes' by Messrs Kellogg. It was fed to orphan lambs by the farmworkers' wives who weeded wheat by hand when chemical weedkillers were still far in the future. This has the same pest and disease dodging advantages as miner's lettuce, though without the crispness and neutral taste that makes it a food for every day like potatoes. The large-leafed type holds 57 mg per 100 g of vitamin C, which leaves greenhouse lettuce standing at the post in winter. Sow it mixed with bonemeal, like *Claytonia*, in March for a crop in May and June which can be cut off with scissors about ½-inch (1 cm) above the neck to grow before the summer sowing in June is ready.

Landcress (*Barbarea praecox*) belongs to the cabbage tribe so can catch clubroot, and can only be eaten by allergy people on the same day as its fellow *Cruciferae* members, but it is very hardy, easy and holds the vitamin C record for January with 82 mg per 100 g. It has almost exactly the taste of watercress and needs to be grown fast for it can be rather strong when it matures. Sow it first in March and the leaves will be ready to snip from its rosettes eight weeks later, as a new taste in summer salads.

Sow celery on window-sills

Celery needs heat to start it, and it is often possible to buy young plants of Golden Self-Blanching to put out in mid May, while the winter varieties can go out as late as June or July, fitting in after early potatoes. Celeriac, the turnip-rooted celery, is impossible to buy as a plant so it is worth raising some plants on a window-sill. Choose one that is really sunny, for light is more important for seedlings than heat, and save for this purpose the plastic containers in which rape or 'cress' is sold by greengrocers in winter, or other narrow trays that will stand in something to catch the surplus from waterings. The easiest soil you can obtain is John Innes Compost, sold in plastic bags from chainstores. This is not compost as known to organic gardeners, but a steam-sterilized potting soil. It will contain superphosphate as well as hoof and horn meal, but at such an early stage in the life of the crop it is not worth bothering about. Levington compost and other all-peat and chemical mixtures mean awkward watering. Purists should search for soil from molehills, which is fine, and pushed up from just below the soil under the turf. This will have weed seeds in it, but otherwise be entirely non-chemical.

Sow the celery and celeriac seed very thinly on the surface of the firmed and flattened soil, and fill the tray in which the containers stand with water so that it is sucked up and moistens the surface. Do this at intervals until the seedlings show celery-shaped leaves. Then transfer to other trays with more space, planting them about 2 inches (5 cm) apart each way. March should be early enough to have them ready for June planting.

While you have seedlings growing on a sunny window-sill (where the celeriac will do the best because it needs less heat than celery), it is a good idea to raise also a herb that is not a hardy perennial. Basil (*Ocimum minimum*) can be sown in March, spaced out like celeriac and planted out in May, 8 inches (20 cm) apart, to grow on in a sunny border and ready to hang up to dry as soon as it flowers before storing in a screw-topped jar.

The most effective aphid hunters are the rather slug-like larvae of hoverflies. Adult hoverflies resemble slender wasps as they dart and poise humming-bird fashion in our gardens, searching for aphid colonies in which they will lay a single egg. Each larvae will eat about 600 aphids before it become an adult, so the more we have the better, especially early in the season.

The adult hoverflies feed on nectar and pollen, but the work of HDRA Members and a team of schoolchildren has established that their favourite annual is *Limnanthes douglasii*, with its yellow and white flowers that earn it the popular name of 'poached egg plant'. Sow it thinly in a sunny place as an edging among the vegetables in March, and again in June for a late crop. It is one of the best bee plants and, though it can seed itself, it is easily destroyed by

The slug-like larvae of the hoverfly are efficient aphid hunters

Above Winter tares, sown before September ends, fix nitrogen through the winter and produce plenty of bulk to dig under in April. 'No digging' gardeners can mow it then set their potatoes on its surface.

Below Essex red clover is the cheapest green manure – its seeds are so small that 1 ounce sows 10 yards (30 g per 9.1 m), mixed with fine bonemeal. Sow in spring to dig under before flowering, or autumn to mow for compost first.

Above Most gardeners only have space for green manure in winter. Grazing rye grows to produce the most bulk to stop plant foods from washing away between sowing in September/October and digging or Rotavating under in April. Also, rabbits dislike it.

Below Annual blue lupins are nitrogen fixers, and have root fungi that make phosphorus available. Sow in May or June as an ideal preparation and dig it in before planting strawberries in August or September.

Above Comfrey is *Symphytum uplandicum*, a hybrid between *S. officinale*, the herbalist's 'knitbone', and *S. asperum*, a Russian species. Lawrence Hills in 1957 with Bocking No. 14 on the HDRA Trial Ground.

Below Its usual use is for making liquid manure for tomatoes and other crops that appreciate its high potassium and magnesium content, for it is so rich in nitrogen that it is an activator rather than a compost material.

Above This favourite garden variety of comfrey has magenta flowers on thin stems entirely unlike those of our wild *S. officinale*. Its value to organic gardeners is in the deep roots that make it a 'mineral mine'.

Below It is a long-lived perennial and its successive cuts through summer make it an excellent mulch under a lawn mowings coat, for bush fruit, especially gooseberries, and tomatoes outdoors or under glass.

hoeing. Even more lovely is *Convolvulus tricolor*, with deep blue saucer-shaped flowers and yellow and white centres, on which fewer hoverflies are seen, because the flowers unfurl early and the flies make a start between 6 and 6.30 am, as timed by a science master Member who did a PhD thesis on these useful flies.

War on wireworms

The wireworm is the larva of the click beetle, of which *Agriotes lineatus* is the most common. It is between ½ and ¾-inch (12-20 mm) long at the pest stage, slender, light brown and with legs and jaws at one end. The adult beetles are no trouble, but in April, May and early June, the 'hens' lay about one hundred eggs each, usually in grass paths and lawns, or anywhere the ground stays undisturbed. At first the larvae are tiny and white, feeding on decayed vegetable matter and preyed on by so many predators that only 15 per cent reach the familiar wireworm size and spend up to four years eating potatoes and carrots, with the roots of leeks, onions, lettuce and tomatoes also popular. Peas and beans are less greedily eaten, though seeds that wait a long time ungerminated in a cold spring can be taken, but parsnips, kale and spinach usually escape.

Wireworms are pests of new gardens and allotments on old pasture land (which often holds eight million wireworms an acre) and neglected gardens. The best way to clear them is by green manuring with mustard. Rake the soil level and either scatter the seed at the rate of 2 ounces a square yard (55 g per 0.83 m²) and rake it in, or sow thinly along furrows 6 inches (15 cm) apart, between the end of March and early May. With an early start, the mustard will be 8 inches (20 cm) high, in bud (not flowering), and ready to dig under by the end of June, before the main July-October feeding period.

Old gardeners and farm-workers used to say that the wireworms fed so greedily on the mustard that they 'busted themselves'. We now know that wireworms spend from two to four years feeding according to the food available, and the mustard foliage 'finishes off' a record crop of beetles which will fly away and lay eggs where some modern farmer will slaughter them expensively with chemicals. A second sowing in July, dug in before the frost, will keep the wireworms eating the mustard rather than your crop. The mustard is of little value as a green manure because it is so soft and sappy.

This drastic counter-attack is not possible in the flower garden where wireworms attack bulbs, especially (it seems) the more expensive lilies, or where they are already doing the damage. They can be trapped during their two feeding periods – from March to mid May and July to October. Cut some perforated zinc into pieces 8 inches (20 cm) long and 6 inches (15 cm) wide, and bend these into cylinders 2 inches (5 cm) in diameter. Lace them along the join with wire, flatten one end and lace this too, and make a wire handle at the other end. Set the traps by filling them with potato or carrot peelings and burying them upright in likely places. Pull them by by the handles every three or four days and dump the catch in the dustbin or chicken run.

The 'black wireworm' is the black millepede (*Tachypodjulus niger*) which coils like a flat watch spring if you pick it up, and feeds on potatoes, carrots and bulbs even more greedily. This creature is not going to change into anything

Wireworm (twice lifesize), the light brown larvae of click beetles

and fly away, and the only defence is trapping; unfortunately it is too fat to get through the perforations in the zinc. Make traps out of tins, fitting these over the end of a stout, round post, and jab holes in the bottom and sides with an old-fashioned tin-opener, or use a power drill with a 3/16-inch bit (or its modern decimal equivalent). Determined trapping round the year will banish these pests, and only the chickens will miss them. Perforated zinc is now scarce and these traps also serve for wireworms.

Fruit care in March
From mid March to mid April is the only time to catch the big bud mite of blackcurrants (*Cecidophyopsis ribis*) out without its 'big bud' on, for it is then that this tiny pest that carries the reversion virus is migrating from the swollen buds which should be picked off whenever they are seen.

Spray with a derris insecticide when the leaves are the size of 5p pieces, which will spare the *Anthocoris* bugs as they do their best to control the mites.

The currant aphid (*Cryptomyzus galeopsidis*) which curls the leaves at the

Black millepedes eat holes in bulbs and tubers. Trapping is the answer

Centipedes eat pests even though they look like pests themselves

tips, making it difficult to kill by spraying, can be caught with soft soap in February or March before the leaves are open to protect it.

Soft soap was once the head gardener's favourite pesticide, but it has been off the market for years after lingering on in ironmongers where it was sold for washing down paint until it was superseded by 'polywhatsanames'. Now it is back, tested and rather tougher in action. There is a big difference between spraying with soapy water or adding soapflakes to help a pesticide to spread through hairs on plants or pests, and genuine soft soap, which is made not with caustic soda, but the equivalents to this from the potash in wood ashes that once washed whitest, from Roman togas to shirts for Samuel Pepys and Beau Brummel's cravats.

Real soft soap is a very selective killer, acting by disrupting the fats in the skins of thin-skinned creatures. This means that it hits all the aphids and spares hard beetles like ladybirds and their leathery-skinned larvae like tiny six-legged crocodiles. It kills thrips and capsids but not the fast scuttling *Anthocoris* bugs and their larvae that feast on mites and their eggs through the winter months on a busy schedule that includes eating lettuce root aphid (*Pemphigus spirothecae*) before it migrates from the poplar trees on which it spends the spring. Now organic gardeners have it again they should make the most of it, starting with the awkward aphid that twists the tips of what would be good strong fruiting shoots on the blackcurrants, and following the pests through the year.

Between the last week in March and mid April is the migration season for the big bud mite of blackcurrants (*Cecidophyopsis ribis*), which can reduce the crop severely but is more feared as a carrier of the reversion virus, for which the only 'cure' is to dig up and burn the

Swollen blackcurrant buds should be picked off. The small bud in the middle is free from big bud mites

days' when they will only visit apples, which makes sure that the pollen from the James Grieve tree gets to the Cox tree with fruitful results. The results of their 'Ribes day' (for gooseberries belong to the same family) are not buds bloated with an internal population explosion. Clusters of buds near the bases of the young shoots will still be brown and dormant at the end of April, which will only have held a few mites, that can still migrate back to the blackcurrants with the reversion virus, even though the other three species resist it.

The symptoms of reversion are longer and narrower leaves, earlier and more brilliant flowering, a poor crop and finally, death, after infecting all the mites for miles. It is useless cutting out attacked shoots as the virus circulates in the sap, so spray all currants *and* gooseberries twice during the season with soft soap, which is cheap, safe for bees and other friends, simple and non-poisonous. The virus is spread only by the mite, so it is safe to dig up the bushes to burn, mites and all in the autumn, and to replant even in the same holes in the spring.

bushes. The usual control is to look over the bare branches, picking off the big buds but some will always be missed to release about five hundred mites a bud, to spread largely by hitch-hiking rides on bees. The mite also attacks red- and whitecurrants and gooseberries too, because bees 'rotate' the flowers they visit, having, for example 'apple

Normal leaf   Diseased leaf

Big bud mites carry the 'reversion' virus of blackberries

CHAPTER 7
APRIL

Table 15: VEGETABLES FOR APRIL EATING

Available for eating	Family	Sowing	Planting
Artichokes, Jerusalem	3	—	February-March
Beans (dried or frozen)	7	May-June	—
Beetroot (stored)	2	May	—
Broccoli (late sprouting)	4	April	June
Cabbage	4	June	July
Carrots (stored)	12	May	—
Celery	12	March-April	May-June
Kale	4	April	June-July
Leeks	8	April	July
Lettuce (winter)	3	August-September	—
Onions (spring)	8	August	—
Onions (stored)	8	March	—
Peas (dried or frozen)	7	January-May	—
Potatoes (stored)	11	—	April-May
Radish, Chinese	4	July	—
Rhubarb	9	April	February
Salsify (leaves)	3	April	—
Spinach (winter)	2	September	—
Sweetcorn (frozen)	6	April-May	—
Tomatoes (bottled)	11	—	May-June

Potato planting

In the south, early potatoes can be sneaked out early in March, but this risks their coming through too soon and getting caught by late frosts. It is better to dig in a green-manure crop or compost and manure first and wait until April with the seed still safe in its chitting trays. On light soils, the quickest and easiest way to plant potatoes is to make 7-inch (18 cm) deep holes with a steel-shod dibber along a garden line, 1 foot (30 cm) apart and 18 inches (45 cm) between rows for earlies and 15 inches (38 cm) apart and 27 inches (68 cm) between rows for maincrop. Then drop the seed tubers down the holes (rose end up) and dibber the soil back over them.

The disadvantage of this method of planting is that it is impossible to place the manure or compost where it will do most good, and on clay soils the dibber puddles the sides till the hole can hold water and either rot the tuber or give it a slow start. Trenching is harder work but as the potatoes are rotated around the garden every bed will have had the benefit of deep digging and deep manuring. It is easy to dig down and find where last year's trenches were and have them in a new place each season.

Dig the trenches 9 inches (23 cm) wide and 1 foot (30 cm) deep to allow room for well-rotted manure or compost on the bottom. This can be the part-rotted surface layers, or any compost that has not heated well, because at this depth weed seeds do no harm. On chalky or sandy soils a layer of leaf-mould on the bottom is an asset to retain moisture. With seed safely chitting it is possible to let the maincrops wait until the first cut of comfrey is ready; leave this to wilt overnight to concentrate, and put 1½-2 pounds (650-900 g) of wilted comfrey to the foot (30 cm) of row, with lawn-mowings in addition, to tread into a 4-inch (10 cm) thick layer.

Whatever method is used, add 2 inches (5 cm) of soil on top, then set out the seed potatoes, eyes up, along it, and fill in with the soil from the next trench. Comfrey alone, or with grass, decays in a kind of long, narrow 'compost heap', releasing plant foods, but also producing humic acids. Potato scab (*Streptomyces scabies*), unlike clubroot, *likes* a limey soil, and the acidity from decay protects the potatoes which stay in the trench. On chalk, where scab is worst, or where heavy liming has been used against clubroot, make the trenches 1 foot (30 cm) wide and deep and use leaf-mould generously (but not last autumn's leaves – they should be the previous autumn's crop).

An intermediate method in terms of work is to dig the bed deeply to the full depth of the fork, leaving a long, straight trench, put 3 inches (8 cm) of compost, manure, or comfrey along it, add about 1 inch (2.5 cm) of soil and then set out the seed. Pile the soil from the next trench on top and dig till the next straight trench comes at the right

spacing. This leaves ridges along the planted potato rows, and it has the advantage that seaweed meal at the rate of 4 ounces a square yard (115 g per 0.83 m²) or rock potash at 8 ounces a square yard (220 g per 0.83 m²) can be dug in at the same time.

If the potatoes come through during a frosty period, draw soil over them with the hoe, or go out after the TV weather forecast and spread newspapers over them, weighed down with canes (for if frost threatens, it will not be windy). When the shoots are 6 inches (15 cm) high and the weeds are starting to grow, draw the soil towards the shoot rows with a swan-neck hoe, the operation known as 'earthing up', which should be done in three stages so you get three kills of seedling weeds before the haulm spreads and takes over weed control. This is why potatoes are called a 'clearing crop'.

Vegetables sowings and care in April

April is the time to sow the slow-maturing cabbage-tribe crops for transplanting. This is best done in a separate seedbed because they are going to fit in after the pea-tribe crops which, especially any for drying, will need their room right up to the last minute. The seedbed need not be in full sun, though this is best, but it must be possible to water it, and it needs 2 pounds a square yard (900 g per 0.83 m²) of lime every other year, holding it at pH 8.5 if you have a soil tester. A good rotation for this bed would be seedlings followed by radishes, summer and winter and drying beans the following season, for the pea tribe love lime, too.

Sow early and late sprouting broccoli, summer cauliflowers, winter cauliflowers (once called 'heading broccoli'), Brussels sprouts, cabbages (summer and winter), and kale, formerly called 'borecole'. Sow all the earlier varieties now, leaving savoys, late-winter and spring cabbages such as April for May sowing. The furrows should be 8 inches (20 cm) apart, and thin sowing is essential, aiming at 2 inches (5 cm) between seeds – not only for economy, because cabbage-tribe seed will keep at least five years, but because uncrowded seedlings make the best plants. Quarter of an ounce (7 g) of any of these mean 2,000 seeds, and most gardeners sow 500 when they want at most fifty.

The seedbed should ideally be large enough to act as a holding area for the Brussels sprouts impatiently waiting for the peas to finish. When the seedlings are 3 inches (8 cm) high, dig them up, snip the tip off the root to make them grow a web of side roots, rather than a single thin taproot, and plant them 4 inches (10 cm) apart each way to wait for moving to their final homes.

The major pest of the cabbage tribe is the cabbage root fly (*Delia brassicae*) and the first hatch from their pupae in the soil is in late April and early May. They hunt by scent and the best way to make sure that the seedlings in the rows or the waiting bed do not have maggots in their roots is to thrust in a 6-foot (2 m) bamboo cane in the middle of the bed and hang a strip of old blanket from it. Then paint a streak of creosote down the blanket, a decoy scent which has been used successfully by organic market gardeners. There are two more hatches, late June to mid-July and August to September, and other measures are needed once the crop is beyond the seedling stage.

The best counter-measure is to cut 8-inch (20 cm) squares of roofing felt, carpet or carpet underlay, with a slit running in to the centre where it is widened to fit the stem. These can be fitted round the cabbages as soon as they are planted, and care should be taken to see they sit flat on the ground and hide the soil: the fly is programmed to lay its eggs just where the stem joins the ground, and this is why even thick polythene is useless. The last hatch of flies can lay eggs on the foliage where they bore into the stems and destroy winter cabbage just when the price is highest. The Scots market gardener who found the cresosote trick has bamboo canes and creosoted blanket strips spaced at 20 feet (6-7 m) intervals each way on a 4-acre (1.6 ha) field, as the cheapest scent masker.

Sow leeks in April so that strong plants are ready to fit in behind the first early potatoes, which are dug as soon as they are in full flower. They do not mind ample lime, so they can be sown with the cabbages in the seedbed, aiming at 1 inch (2.5 cm) between the quite large seeds. Those who want to eat leeks in September and November can sow a fast kind like Early Market, while a slow one to outlast Musselbugh is Sutton's Winter Crop to extend the season until the end of April. Though leeks and onions are a useful source of sulphur, their main dietary value is the vitamin A in the leaves, so merely shorten these to half length instead of trimming away the best part as greengrocers will.

Spinach family problem

The taste of spinach comes from oxalic acid, and though New Zealand spinach is in a natural order all on its own, it has about a third as much as the summer spinach in the shoot tips which are eaten. It has the advantage of supplying spinach all the summer without the constant resowing that summer spinach needs to keep up a supply. New Zealand spinach (*Tetragonia expansa*) can be sown in the open in April, or May in the north. It is slow to germinate, so should be soaked in cold water overnight and sown in threes, spaced a foot (30 cm) apart each way, and thinned to the best in each cluster when all are up and thriving.

Start picking when the sprawling,

fleshy, shoots are 6 inches (15 cm) long, and take about 3 inches (8 cm) of stem and dark-green arrowhead leaves from each, and keep on picking from June until the frost kills it. It will seed itself from the insignificant flowers along the stems, and it pays to leave it to grow of its own accord every year. It is tastiest when constantly picked, and if a guest-house or nature clinic could keep on top of the production of one 12-foot (4 m) row, the yield would be fantastic.

The best of the spinach family is Swiss chard, a beetroot grown for its leaves and which has wide, heavy mid-ribs, sometimes cooked separately, that can be 4 inches (10 cm) wide. There are a number of varieties of which Lucullus is the hardiest green, and Ruby or Rhubarb, a striking red and a favourite with flower arrangers. Sow in April or May in clusters of three (thinned to the best) 1 foot (30 cm) apart with 15 inches (38 cm) between rows to allow room for walking between and twisting off the leaves that can be 18 inches (45 cm) long, as well as hoeing. These are for summer eating.

Spinach beet, or perpetual spinach, will also produce a supply of green food from July into the autumn, even right round until April from an August sowing. Sow the large seeds in pairs 1 foot (30 cm) apart in 1 inch-deep (2.5 cm) dibber holes with 15 inches (38 cm) between rows. Pick the leaves by bending them down until they break off, not cutting or pulling in case they bleed. Cut off any flower stems that grow in summer and never strip a plant – sow plenty to share the burden. Summer spinach, if required for salads, should be sown at three-week intervals from March until the last in September, each sowing taking about five weeks to grow from seed and offering three weeks'

Table 16: COMPARATIVE LEVELS OF OXALIC ACID IN LONG-SEASON VEGETABLES

	Calcium (per cent)	Oxalic acid (per cent)
Chenopodium album (the weed fat-hen)	0.0990	1.1100
young leaves	—	0.052
Spinach, ordinary	0.1330	0.8920
Beetroot leaves	0.1200	0.9160
New Zealand spinach (leaves)	0.1100	0.8900
Seakale beet (chard) leaves	0.1100	0.6600
Seakale beet (chard) midribs	0.0450	0.2900
New Zealand spinach (stems)	0.0830	0.6500
New Zealand spinach (tips)	—	0.3400
Parsley	0.2900	0.1900
Beetroot (unpeeled)	0.0180	0.1380
Broccoli	0.2100	0.0054
Kale	0.3100	0.0130
Cabbage	0.1890	0.0077
Carrots	0.0440	0.0330
Lettuce	0.0730	0.0071
Rhubarb (cooked stems)	0.0440	0.5000

Table 17: NUTRITIONAL COMPOSITION OF LONG-SEASON VEGETABLES

	A	C	E	Niacin	Thiamine	Riboflavin
	(IUs)	Mg per 100g			µg per 100g	
Spinach, ordinary	8,400-25,000	59-75	1.70	0.70 0.20	50,120	240-300
Spinach New Zealand	1,400	62.50	0.20	1-1	1-1	1-1
Chenopodium	19,000	85	1.80	1.00	59	690
Beetroot leaves	21,000	34-50	1-1	0.30	50	170-300
Carrots	10,000	6-10	1-1	1.50	60-70	60
Kale	7,000-20,000	100	8.00	0.80	120	350-500

picking before it bolts.

The problem of these useful, long-season vegetables, with hardly any pests or diseases, is their oxalic acid level shown in Table 16. Unfortunately, breeding for a low oxalic acid level, when this is what they are intentionally grown for, is as unrewarding as designing a silent transistor radio. Rhubarb leaves are so high in oxalic acid that there have been poisoning cases, but there has never been a case of spinach poisoning, and only vegans, or those on a milk-free or other low-calcium diet, risk shortage. On the other hand, it would be risky to live entirely on beetroot leaves. In 1948, refugees in Dresden, Berlin and Leipzig were treated in hospital for oxalic poisoning and liver damage from excessive vitamin A, after living for several weeks on cooked *Chenopodium album* growing on the rubble of bombed buildings. The answer is to eat beetroot roots and not leaves and not to make anything your sole diet.

Nutritionally this group of vegetables is valuable, as shown in Table 17, but in vegetables vitamin A is present as Carotene, which is converted by the liver into the vitamin. In the case of *Chenopodium* beetroot leaves and spinach, this is far higher even than in carrots, and can be a great strain on the liver. A fashion for beetroot-leaf eating, like glue sniffing, would be a serious health risk. Young *Chenopodium* leaves gathered in the spring however, have little more oxalic acid than kale.

Sweetcorn and pumpkins

In our climate, we can grow sweetcorn for eating on the cob if we choose a fast kind like Sutton's First of All. We can enjoy it freshly picked from the end of August, and then from the deep freeze, and the bulk of compost material it grows is a welcome bonus. Sweetcorn, or maize, is greedy for phosphorus, and purple streaks on the leaves are the sign of shortage. Sweetcorn is a pleasant rest for a cabbage-weary soil, but do look over the bed in April for any seedlings of *Chenopodium*, not only to eat when it is young and tasty, but to see if it is pink or even pale, red-purple round the growing point. This is a certain sign of phosphorus shortage and it is also worth checking a new strawberry bed before planting, for strawberries also demand phosphorus. If fish meal is available, spread 4 ounces a square yard (115 g per 0.83 m²) before digging ready for sowing, and if not scatter 8 ounces (220 g) of fine bonemeal instead.

Sow the large seeds 1 inch (2.5 cm) deep, making a depression with the trowel to hold water, 15 inches (38 cm) apart and 2 feet (60 cm) between rows, then cover each with a polythene bag 'cloche'. These are made with two 18-inch (45 cm) lengths of 20-gauge galvanised iron wire, bent into a giant hairpin about 4 inches (10 cm) wide; thrust the ends of the wires into the ground across the seed so it makes a 'croquet hoop' about 4 inches (10 cm) high, and set the other one across it. Pull a small polythene bag down over the hoops with a rubber band round the bottom to prevent it blowing away.

Wire coathangers are good for making these cloches, and save you quite a sum which can be better spent on cobs and compost. You can also make them larger, large enough to sneak tomatoes under. You can also leave the frames in place when it is warm and put the bags back on them when frost threatens. Water the depression under the 'cloche' and, because the sun on the polythene will warm the weeds ahead as well as the corn, after two weeks remove the bags, weed and inspect your corn. When the shoot is 3 inches (8 cm) long, remove the bags and wire and let the corn grow, storing the bags and wires for the next season. Sweetcorn can be sown in May without cloches, but it gains from the flying start.

Polythene-bag cloches give the same gain in growing time for pumpkins, marrows, courgettes and outdoor cucumbers, which can also be sown in March if there is room on a sunny window-sill and the care and attention to keep them watered in their plastic pots of John Innes compost. Plant these out in mid April, but protect them from

Wire coathangers make hoops for polythene bag cloches and runner bean hooks.

frosts and cold winds for the first few nights by spreading a cardboard carton over each, with its flaps spread and weighed down with stones.

Pumpkins have shoots that race for long distances and they will not fit into a neat rotation. They should go on rough ground that needs something to cover it and that will hold down weeds. Dig holes 5 feet (1.5 m) apart each way, and 1 foot (30 cm) square and deep. Fill

POLYTHENE BAG 'CLOCHE' FOR PUMPKINS AND CUCUMBERS

these half full of trodden, rough compost or leafmould and kitchen waste, topped with replaced soil packed down to leave a 1 inch-deep (2.5 cm) depression round each, which can be filled with water by hose if the pumpkins flag in drought. Take off the cartons when the weather is friendly and let the pumpkins run. When each shoot has grown at least one plain stemmed male flower and one female, with a miniature round pumpkin behind it, cut the shoot off after this female flower. If such trimming can be kept up this should mean more moderate-sized pumpkins to store and fewer monsters for weight guessing in aid of Oxfam.

Modern outdoor cucumbers are far nicer than the old rough skinned type. Grow them on the same system, but with holes only 3 feet (1 m) apart each way, remembering, however, that unlike the pumpkins, they cannot be stored for winter use. This applies also to marrows and courgettes, both as bush types for the 3-foot (1 m) spacing. Marrows can be left to grow woody by those who want to make marrow jam,

but if they are allowed to mature like pumpkins they will keep, but they can no longer be cooked as a vegetable.

Courgettes need picking every other day, but are value for room if you can keep pace with them and are delicious sliced and lightly stir-fried. They will grow well spaced 4 feet (1.2 m) apart each way, planted in trowel holes through an allotment-reclaiming carpet, which starts cropping sooner, and a single plot would supply enough for a health food shop to sell.

The radishes between the parsnips will have finished and as they take about twenty days from seed to salad, sowing-thinly in pairs of furrows 2 inches (5 cm) apart about every three weeks will keep up the supply. Radishes are in and out of the soil so fast they escape clubroot and can fit in like extra sowings of lettuce wherever there is room. A second sowing of early peas should go in now, early, because the maincrops need high and costly sticks but anything only 18 inches (45 cm) or 2 feet (60 cm) tall can be cheaply supported.

It is possible to cut relatively short branching sticks in the country and it is far easier to thrust them in along the rows than to find anything taller than 2 feet (60 cm). Stout nylon net can be bought up to this height, and wire netting about 2 feet (60 cm) tall stretched round posts at the end of the rows, and held upright by canes thrust down the sides, doubles as support and protection from birds for peas that have outgrown their guards. The netting lasts for years if it is unhooked and rolled up to store in a shed at the end of the season.

Pest control in April
Pea seedlings can develop 'scalloped edges' to their young leaves in some gardens and so can broad beans due to attacks by the pea and bean weevil (*Sitonia lineatus*). In April the larvae are

eating the nodules on the new roots of your seedlings, which does more damage than adults nibbling the leaves. Another hidden pea and bean pest is the bean seed fly (*Delia platura*), related to the onion fly. This feeds on the roots of pea-tribe seedlings in March and April, normally doing little harm, but in cold springs when root growth is slow, it can slaughter whole rows. For both pests, water along the rows with the cigarette-end nicotine solution (see page 53), using a rosed watering can and soaking close to the seedlings. You will not see any effect on the surface but your seedlings may recover. The solution's effectiveness will be spent in 48 hours, and it does not appear to kill earthworms.

Anthocoris is the natural controller of gooseberry mite (*Bryobia*) attacking in April and May in dry weather, turning the leaves grey with loss of sap so they drop early and starve the fruit. Spray with soft soap or paraffin emulsion to help your plants catch up on the pest. Strawberry aphid (*Chaetosiphon fra-*

gaefolii) hatches first in April and this winged generation can be killed, before they spread, with soft soap, so it is worth watching for pale green or light yellow aphids on the undersides of the leaves. This is why it is essential to use predator-safe pesticides – ladybirds and *Anthocoris* have sharper eyes and more time than we have to hunt for these virus spreaders through spring and summer.

It is no longer necessary to smear sticky material on to greaseproof-paper bands and tie them round the trees, for modern greases can be safely painted on the bark, and there is no risk that determined wingless female winter moths (*Operophtera brumata*) will find a subway under it along a hollow in the trunk, for older trees may not be perfectly round. Inspect the grease to make sure no twig or leaf has blown against it and stuck to form a bridge, and renew the mixture to stop the summer traffic up your trees.

CHAPTER 8

MAY

Table 18: VEGETABLES FOR MAY EATING

Available for eating	Family	Sowing	Planting
Beans (dried or frozen)	7	May-June	—
Beetroot (stored)	2	May	—
Broccoli (late sprouting)	4	April	June
Cabbage	4	June	July
Carrots (stored)	12	May	—
Kale	4	April	June-July
Leeks	8	April	July
Lettuce (winter)	3	August-September	—
Onions (spring)	8	August	—
Onions (stored)	8	March	—
Peas (dried or frozen)	7	January-May	—
Potatoes (stored)	11	—	April-May
Radishes	4	March-August	—
Rhubarb	9	April	February
Spinach (summer)	2	February	—
Sweetcorn (frozen)	6	April-May	—
Tomatoes (bottled)	11	—	May-June

Tomato plant time

Once it was possible to buy tomato plants raised in heat with a choice of varieties, but the loss of the passenger-train parcels service forces us to take whatever the local garden centre sells, or to grow our own. Harbinger, the best early ripener with a thin skin and a real taste can be raised on a window-sill, in a box of John Innes seed soil, covered with a sheet of glass turned every morning to take away the condensation, and removed when the seedlings appear. Pot them, when real tomato leaves show between the two pointed seed leaves, and keep them growing on the window-sill till about the second week in May. The plants will be smaller than bought ones, about 6 inches (15 cm) high, but commercial plants are grown to greenhouse planting size, which is on the large side for outdoors.

Some gardens have a single sunny border where the tomatoes must go each year, and this can be rotated with cucumbers and runner beans, with a green manure crop sown each winter and dug in each spring. The best policy is to rotate them round with the vegetables, ideally following the sprouting broccoli which come out as they go in.

Dig holes for the plants, like those for

pumpkins, 2 feet (60 cm) apart and 3 feet (1 m) between rows to allow room for trimming, tying and picking. Put 2 inches (5 cm) of leafmould on the bottom of the hole, add 4 inches (10 cm) of compost and fill up with soil, treading these firm and leaving a ½-inch (1 cm) deep depression on top. This will deepen as the compost and leafmould sink, but as tomatoes grow larger they will need to trap water from can or hose. Drive in a stake in the centre of each hole because if it goes in when the plants are large and waiting for it, this may damage the roots.

Ideally, you need a 5-foot (1.5 m) dahlia stake, for it must stand about 4 feet (1 m) above ground, but height is expensive these days. Reject broom-handles can sometimes be bought; dahlia stakes are good but expensive, and ordinary 1 by 1 inch (2.5 cm) timber, pointed and sawn to sizes is cheaper. It is essential to coat any stake with creosote or other wood preservative, because the watering means that bare wood rots at ground level and soon your stakes are too short to use.

Put out the plants, taking care not to break the soil ball, water well, then open out a colour supplement magazine and secure it to the stake with drawing pins. This will keep the wind off the plant and protect it from frost for the first week after planting, but should be burnt or thrown in the dustbin when the plants are safe in the open, because glazed paper composts badly, though supplements last better in the open than popular periodicals of the same size. Tie a short length of non-nylon string first round the stake and then round the young plant as a first support.

Celery and celeriac

Self-blanching celery for the summer needs no trenches. Spread a bucketful of compost to the square yard or metre and dig over the bed before spacing out the bought or window-sill-raised plants, 1 foot (30 cm) apart and 18 inches (45 cm) between rows, making a depression round each to hold water, both to start them and for when they need watering in drought. Ordinary celery can be planted in May, but as it is demanding in space it can wait till late June or July when the early potatoes come out and release room.

By mid May, each of the seedling celeriac should have a slight bulge at the base ready to earn it the name of 'turnip rooted celery'. Plant them like the Golden Self-Blanching celery with the bulge at ground level and give them a well-watered start. Hoe them, like the celery, and their stem bases will swell on the surface until they look like turnips with celery tops. Remove any sideshoots that appear and by October they can weigh as much as 3 pounds (1.3 kg) each. Grate them raw in salads through the winter and treat them like kohlrabi, the other swollen-stem vegetable that is also unappreciated. They can be lifted, the tops removed, and then stored as root vegetables, but it is better to earth them up with mature leafmould as a winter protection.

May is a better time to sow beetroot for winter storage than March; June is not too late, but the May sowing brings the cricket-ball sizes that keep well and give a worthwhile supply of food from the space. Chantenay Red Cored carrots, or Sutton's Favourite (a larger form of Chantenay) for winter storage are also best sown at the same spacing as the earlies, but towards the end of this month. This sowing will be ready for thinning when the first carrot fly attack is over, but it may suffer from the August and September onslaught.

Countering carrot fly

The carrot fly (*Psila rosae*) belongs to the same family as the cabbage-root fly, and the traditional remedies rely on masking this scent with something stronger. Planting carrots next to onions, scattering lawn-mowings between the rows at fortnightly intervals to maintain a barrage of hay scent, soaking sawdust in paraffin and sprinkling it along the rows and winding string round short stakes, dipping this in creosote and thrusting them in at intervals, all have their advocates confident of success, but they also have their failures.

They probably are effective on carrot flies homing in on the thinnings from the maximum range of seven miles, five miles or even a mile, but when the pupae are hatching in the garden next door, the flies use their eyes. One new and quite effective method developed on the HDRA Trial Ground is to surround a 3-foot (1 m) wide and 12-foot (4 m) long carrot bed with clear polythene, ideally 16-inch (40 cm) wide tubing with a string along the top and bottom edges to stretch it firmly round four stout corner posts. Stapling over the string rather than the polythene prevents the wind tearing it away. The treated plots inside the polythene curtain gave a 47 per cent yield increase compared with the plots without polythene which had 29.2 per cent carrot fly-damaged roots compared with 10.8 per cent for the protected plots.

This method has proved so effective that Papronet (a fine mesh polythene material) is now sold as an anti-carrot fly screen and is also used to make tunnel cloche coverings that let through rain and air but exploit the 'greenhouse effect' that gives the increased yield. The cabbage-root fly (*Delia brassicae*) and the onion fly (*D. antiqua*), however, are not baffled by the new invention. The traditional carpet underlay or felt squares fitted round the stem protect the cabbages, and the onion fly needs different solutions.

The popularity of modern improved onion sets nearly drove seed varieties off the market because they needed no thinning so did not broadcast the scent of onion foliage that draws the flies up to five miles away. Wild leeks, onions and garlic are relatively rare, unlike hemlock and cow parsley, which maintain the stock of carrot flies, and the onion fly might easily have joined the last British wolf and great auk (last sighted in 1844.) The descendants of the onion flies that were capable of homing in on unbruised onion leaves are now increasing fast.

The pupae overwinter less deeply than those of the carrot fly, and hoeing, rather than digging, the surface of the plot where the onions were attacked by 5/16 inch (8 mm) long white maggots in January, February or March, will feed many to the robins. The onion fly produces three generations a year, and the later hatches, which only have to use their eyes to find their food, can build up a large population very quickly. They lay their eggs near the sets or seedlings, so the best counter-measure is either topless and bottomless food tins, taller than those used against cut worms, or jars taller than 1 pound (0.45 kg) jam or honey jars, with the bottoms removed by pouring in boiling water, which cracks them off. These are the best and the old 2 pound (0.9 kg) jam jars ideal, fitted over the growing set or thinned seedling, and removed in July to let in the sun for ripening and drying.

Sow drying peas in May
The tall but early Pilot peas for drying, with White Achievement and any other white-seeded runner beans to pick green or dry, should be sown or planted in May. It is possible to steal a march on the year by sowing the peas singly in pots or yogurt cartons with ½-inch (1 cm) holes melted in the bottoms and set on sand in watertight trays on window-sills, to plant out in May from March sowings. Runner beans are more

robust, and setting out the seeds 2 inches (5 cm) apart each way in a tray full of leafmould, in March and keeping them watered on a window-sill allows them to be planted in May rather than sown. The cost of a small greenhouse or even a frame is so high today that, in view of the fact that it is only of value for three months – February, March and April, the gain in time and crop is not enough to balance the cost and trouble of the many plastic substitutes for pots and seedtrays and the heating and upkeep. Window-sills win!

The best support for Pilot is metre-wide wire netting (the wider the mesh the cheaper), supported on stout stakes at each row end, like those of normal peas. Because they will not be picked, the rows can be 18 inches (45 cm) instead of 30 inches (75 cm) apart, which still allows space for hoeing. Pick some of the lower pods for eating but when the leaves start yellowing and the oldest pods wrinkle and split, withhold water and let them dry slowly. When the oldest pods gape it is time to pull up the stakes, cut off the stems at ground level, lay them on polythene in the sun to ripen, beat them with a stick when the pods are crisp and pull the haulm off the netting for compost. The peas for eating in soups and stew through the winter can be stored in polythene sweet-jars or anything airtight, but those for next year's seed should go into paper envelopes in a dry drawer because they need to breathe. Drying your own peas is an unfashionable art, and therefore it is no longer possible to buy such old drying varieties as Harrison's Glory through seedsmen. The way round the regulations is to buy from a supermarket a packet of dry green peas, which will probably be Maro, Proco or Alaska only sold on contract to farmers, and sow it in March, April or May. It will be a heavier crop but not as fast as Pilot, and may well be tastier for it was bred

to hold its flavour when dried.

Sugar peas should be gathered young to eat pods and all, but they are better still when grown to pick for raw eating in salads. They are extra sweet, and contain about five times the amount of vitamin C, three times the riboflavin, and four times as much thiamine as canned or frozen.

The tall variety of sugar pea, with dark and light blue flowers, dries sweetest and well. So does the tallest of all maincrops, Alderman, which will climb 6 feet (1.8 m), producing a very heavy crop for drying.

Beans in May

Runner beans are taller still and need 8-foot (2.5 m) bamboo canes, set out as in the illustration (see page 46). Using pairs of canes in inverted 'V's every 4 feet (1.2 m), instead of every 8 inches (20 cm), and filling in with strings led down to metal skewers from the cross-canes at the top, saves money, for string is cheaper. The canes should spread about a foot (30 cm) at the bottom, and the beans be sown or planted in a double row along the sides of the 1 foot-wide (30 cm) trench. Few families need more than a single 12-foot (4 m) row of runners, because the yield depends on how closely they are picked. Take the large, low pods first and just pick for eating and freezing from even a dozen plants.

Drying beans are grown in the same way, but without picking, and as they run higher and flop over above the canes, cut the upper growth and small pods with the shears for compost material to put more strength into the driers. These should be picked when they are light brown and split easily, ready to set out in the potato chitting trays which are stacked on top of each other to finish drying. Another way to grow drying beans is from vine-eyes (like big screw-eyes in rawlplugs) as high up the side of the house as your steps will reach, or you can twist one into a bedroom window-sill. Runner beans were originally imported as ornamental climbers for Chatsworth-size greenhouses, and they are twiners round strings, rather than tendril clingers like peas. So they will go 15 or even 20 feet (5-6 m) up strings held down by metal skewers in a rubbish-filled bean-trench below a windowless wall. If you have two suitable positions, alternate them with *Tropaeolum peregrinum*, the bright yellow-flowered canary creeper, or *Ipomaea purpurea*, the hardiest of the morning glories, as two good, climbing, hardy annuals which will offer a mass of compost material when the strings are cut in the autumn; the beans offer all this and food too. The best runner bean for drying is the Czar, which has white flowers and seeds exactly like rather smaller butter beans, but with a nicer flavour than any on sale in packets today. Second choice is White Achievement, a climbing French bean which produces haricot sizes.

French beans
French beans have only the family and the deep freeze to keep pace with, so you need fewer than you think. Start picking when the pods are only 4 inches (10 cm) long and never let them grow large and yellow, for then they cease production and ripen what they have. Their trenches should be 8 inches (20 cm) apart, and the beans go 6 inches (15 cm) apart and 2 inches (5 cm) deep.

Purley King is the best drier, with Romano runner up. Horsehead, the best of all, has hit EEC trouble, because the patent fees cripple a variety that has been bred for the relatively few people who want to dry their own. The seed trade is now where publishing would be if books were taxed, with the same rate for bestsellers as first volumes of poems, and no firm would print anything but

TV linked works to sell millions. We may yet come to this.

In dry springs and almost always on sandy soils, seedlings of the cabbage family, especially radishes and turnips, have their young leaves eaten into lace by the small, black, skipping flea beetles (*Phyllotreta species*) of which there are about five that appear in gardens. The usual answer is to dust with derris. Derris is made from the ground root of *Derris elliptica*, a fish poison plant used in Malaya that is harmless to warm-blooded animals. This is safe for people, pets and wildlife, but not goldfish, bees and insect predators. It is spent in 48 hours, it does not build up along the chains of eaters and eaten to dangerous levels as would the synthetic 'organo' pesticides, and it does not select resistant strains of the pests against which it is sprayed. Flea beetles have no natural enemies hunting them along our radish rows, where no bees or ladybirds fly, so use it freely. Unfortunately it does not kill slugs.

Flea beetles winter in rubbish along hedges and the hiding places generously provided by the countryside and even untidy gardens, and they can fly up to a kilometre in search of seedlings. If you suffer every year from flea-bitten brassicas, it is worth sowing a thin belt of mustard round the cabbage-tribe seedbed because the flea beetles are reputed to prefer the taste. This trap-cropping idea would not be traditional if it did not work well enough to be worth the trouble.

Sow the second batch of cabbage-tribe plants towards the end of the month, extra lettuces and another batch of lamb's lettuce and miner's lettuce for those who must have constant changes in their salads. Keep up the lettuce sowings, thinning and transplanting to stretch each one over six weeks. Watch for small holes in radish and cabbage plant seedlings, which will be caused by the flea beetle, small, black and skipping, for which derris dust is the best answer.

Organic fruit care in May

In May the apple capsid (*Plesiocoris rugicollis*) and the green capsid (*Lygus pabulinus*) – tubby little bugs about ¼-inch (7 mm) long – may be seen running about leaves on sunny days in May and June. They are quite distinct from aphids because they are faster, larger and greedier. The answer for the apple capsids, which suck the leaves surrounding the blossom so that the fruitlets develop corky patches, is to hose the trees, squirting the water up high and hard. The disturbance shakes the capsids down as rain rarely does, and as they are wingless they get caught on the grease-band round the trunk, renewed in April.

The green capsid attacks gooseberries, currants, raspberries and roses, but unfortunately these cannot be grease-banded. Paint two lengths of hardboard about 1 foot (30 cm) wide and 1 yard (0.9 m) long with the grease-band material, slide these one on each side of the gooseberry, currant or rose bush, and either shake the bush or hose or syringe with force. The grease is water-proof and the boards may last another season, if protected with other sheets of hardboard, but separated by nailing strips of wood round the sides and ends. The raspberry beetle is out laying eggs in the blossom on sunny days in May and June and to spray with anything strong enough to kill a beetle means killing bees. One way round is to set the greased boards on each side of the row, on a dull day when the beetles will not be flying but resting and crawling, and shake the canes so they fall on to the grease. Two people sliding the boards along and shaking can go over a raspberry bed almost as fast as if they were spraying with something deadly.

The raspberry weevil (*Otiorhyncus picipes*) is nocturnal and the best control is to go out with the boards at night and shine a powerful torch along the canes to deceive the weevils into thinking it is time to drop quickly and go home to bed under clods or in a mulch. This creature, sometimes called the 'clay coloured weevil', also attacks gooseberries, apples, damsons and strawberries, eating young blossom and leaves as well as attacking the bark on young shoots. In orchards switch on the light of a large torch *suddenly*. Spread newspapers if you want to hear them patter down, but coating these with grease is too time-consuming and costly, and entirely unnecessary; the weevils are wingless and are caught by the grease bands, which can have the surface scraped off and given a fresh coat if there is a bad weevil epidemic (they are rumoured to be producing organo-chlorine resistant varieties). There are a number of other weevils that can be controlled in the same way, and there is no need to bother about the names, for if anything is walking about in your trees at night it is up to no good. *Anthocoris* mites are not nocturnal and cling on tighter in bark crevices; the adults are winged and can fly back. Some weevils fly, but reluctantly, for they are rather under-engined for their weight.

There is no room in this book to describe these pests and their life cycles, only the organic remedies where these exist. The scientific names are given so that descriptions can be checked in standard reference works from libraries. They may be off-putting for beginners, but there is no law of nature that says beginners only get pests with simple answers and easy names.

In the past chickens were kept in orchards partly as pest eaters. Work at East Malling in the 1940s showed that chickens are less efficient than ducks. The newly popular Welsh Harlequin breed, which lays eggs with white 'whites' almost identical with hens' eggs, are the best slug-eaters of all. Protect seedlings with wire pea-guards and let the ducks roam the gardens.

Geese graze orchards, and too many of them will eat everything but the plantains, but they are grazing birds and not of value as pest controllers. Ducks and chickens (especially bantams, which offer more beaks and keen pairs of eyes to the pound of supplementary food) are at their most valuable between the beginning of May and the end of September. There would be scope for an organic poultry farmer to run the flock on deep litter or straw yard with artificial lighting from September till April, and in an old-fashioned wheeled house moved occasionally in an orchard. This would increase the tiny total of *genuine* free-range eggs sold in Britain today.

The lackey moth has hairy caterpillars up to 1½ inches (4 cm) long, blue-grey with reddish and white stripes, devouring leaves and shoots. They spin web nests on branch forks or knit together leaves in which they hide from sprays and their natural enemy which is the cuckoo – out early in orchards to hear the munching of the first caterpillar. Once these nests were destroyed by firing a muzzle-loading gun at them with a reduced charge of powder and paper wads. Destroy the nests when they are small, but spray with nicotine in early May before the caterpillars start to spin. The eggs are laid in bands round the smaller mature branches, each of which can hold as many as 200 in July and August. Cut off these branches, unless they are good, healthy spurs, or smash them with the secateurs. These eggs are immune to winter washes and so the pest is increasing.

Pruning stone fruit

May is the time to start pruning stone fruit such as peaches, nectarines and apricots. Go over them first for 'dieback', which is caused by a number of fungi that begin by attacking dead wood from frost or bullfinch damage, and go on to attack the living tissue, like canker in apples or pears. Snip off the dead end of any shoot and snip again and again until the wood shows clean, with no brown stain in the middle. This has the same tonic effect on the tree that extracting a decaying tooth has on a human being, and newly planted stone fruits should not be cut back to shape them at planting time like apples, but left till May in case any damage done when moving them has caused dieback.

Peaches can fruit on small spurs, but mostly on the long shoots that grew the previous year. Tie these and their older companions into the wires, if they are growing on a wall (as they usually are). When they have fruited, wait till the following May and cut them back to three or four buds – whichever points along the wall – and tie in the shoots when they are young and bendy. Another type of shoot rushes straight up, thick and strong, from the base, and this should be cut right back to the first sideways-pointing bud; this is the policy for any shoot that points awkwardly out away from the wall. If you want to cover the wall, the fruited shoots should be left alone to grow from the tips. This means fruit further and further from the centre of the fan, while hard pruning means more in the middle.

Give the first thinning at pruning time, removing one from each pair of fruitlets so they are not more than 6 inches (15 cm) apart all over the tree. Thinning is important because while good varieties should fruit every year, those that are raised from stones get about eight years' rest until there is a spring gentle enough to miss the blossom. Apricots flower earliest of all, and the reason many of the old walled gardens of England had walls built double, with chimneys along them, was so that rubbish could be burned between to warm the brick from inside in the days when head gardeners relied on instinct and the look of the frosty stars rather than well-dressed TV weather experts hanging warning discs on isobar-lined maps.

Plums and greengages produce their fruiting spurs on one- and two-year-old shoots, therefore if you cut them back like apples you are cutting away the crop. Newly planted trees need no pruning other than the routine dieback search in May. When they are trained on walls (greengages do very well on north- or even east-facing walls), tie the fan-trained branches to the wires with non-nylon string and pinch back any side shoots that point outwards to two or three buds – whichever points along the wall. If one of the leading shoots intrudes on a window, or a branch no longer fruits, cut it out in May, but do not keep taking out the fruited two-year-old shoots as with peaches, apricots and nectarines.

Bush and standard plums need only anti-dieback snipping, and sawing out crowded or crossing branches in May. On a Victoria plum that is growing too large for a small garden, it is safe to shorten the main leades to 12 inches (30 cm) and the side shoots to 8 inches (20 cm) in June, as a kind of summer pruning. Even if branches break with a heavy harvest, do not saw them out until the safe season in May and June.

Victorias are the most popular and tasty plum variety, but they have long branches that break. The best policy is to buy bush, rather than standard, trees, and make stout, wooden, inverted 'V's with a good crossing crotch at the top to fit the branches. A heavy branch is a powerful lever when it is covered with fruit, and propping it reduces the length and provides a second fulcrum, so it will not tear the main branch away.

Pest control in May

The banning of nicotine (safe for so many predators, on the grounds that it is a danger to human beings, even though it is vastly safer than cigarettes) has set organic gardeners looking for the safest substitutes to spare our friends and harm only our foes. I am constantly searching for answers that depend on cunning rather than chemicals, however safe, but I have to give the best answer I can to the orthodox amateur who demands to know, 'What would *you* do if thousands of caterpillars were stripping the leaves off your fruit bushes?'

The gooseberry sawfly caterpillar (*Nematus ribesii*) hatches from buried cocoons in April and the small green caterpillars with black heads and spots from eggs laid along the leaf veins, can strip all the leaves off a gooseberry or currant bush in five days. They feed for a month, drop to the ground, pupate and are back in time to fit three generations into a summer. If they have killed your bushes, the later sawfly crops can fly several miles with a following wind.

The magpie moth (*Abraxas grossulariat*) specializes in bush fruit but also attacksapricots, cherries and plums. Watch for small yellow, black and white 'looper' caterpillars up to 1½ inches (40 mm) long between April and June, which feed furiously for about a month, develop into black- and yellow-banded pupae in cocoons on leaves, twigs and even fences, hatching to black and white moths flying in late July and August to fresh currants and gooseberries with enough leaves to strip and feed next year's caterpillars hibernating through the winter.

If you have kept your bush fruit mulched, shallow forking up of the mulch after the leaves have fallen will expose the small sawfly pupae to your local robins. If there is a way of feeding the common wren (*Troglodytes troglodytes troglodytes*, the longest scientific name for one of the smallest British birds) selectively, more would come through every winter and eat more of the shallow sleeping pupae. The magpie moth just flutters in for sudden slaughter then makes its getaway.

Organic gardeners have long relied on the dried flowers of *Chrysanthemum cinerarifolium* (pyrethrum) and the ground root of a Malayan fish poison plant (derris) as 'safe' pesticides because they do not build up along food chains and are harmless to warm-blooded creatures including humans, birds and animals and domestic pets, except tortoises, toads and goldfish. The active principals in both have been investigated, synthesized and made more deadly. In 1978 it was discovered that even natural pyrethrum is 25 times as poisonous to bees as DDT, though some of the synthetic variations are three times as deadly and last two months rather than for twenty-four hours as do the natural, which allowed gardeners to spray their few trees in the evening after the bees had gone to bed, and be more than half spent before they were working on the blossom in the morning. Derris is safe for bees, but the synthetic version of this natural alkaloid is likely to select resistant variations of pests, and is a killer for all garden friends. It is an emergency answer for large caterpillars now that the ladybird is safe and the quickly spent nicotine has been banned.

Derris and pyrethrum were often used as a mixture, killing more effectively together than separately. Soft soap has the same 'synergizing' effect with quassia chips that make an old-fashioned weak insecticide for aphids, small caterpillars and mites, sparing bees, ladybirds and larvae, hoverfly larvae and *Anthocoris*. Simmer 1 ounce (28 g) of the chips in a litre of rainwater for an hour, topping up as the water boils away, stir in 1 ounce (28 g) of soft soap and dilute with 3½ pints (2 l) of water. Spray against apple and plum sawflies (*Hoplocampa testudinea* and *H. flava*) a week after petal fall to catch the tiny caterpillars before they are safe inside the fruitlets and you will spare the bees that will still be about. It is not possible to time later sprayings to catch these caterpillars as they move from fruit to fruit (three apples or four plums before they reach maturity.) Nor can they be destroyed by picking up windfalls. When the caterpillars are fully fed they drop from the fruit and overwinter in cocoons underground. In the past, when chickens were kept in the orchards, from mid June to the end of July they were very useful pest controllers.

The quassia and soap mixture is the bee- and predator-safe spray against gooseberry and currant sawfly, and the pear midge (*Contarina pyrivorus*), which is responsible for pear fruitlets growing extra large and falling in May and June full of tiny maggots. Collect all these windfalls for burning or dustbin dumping or spray with soap and quassia when the buds show white and again when these are fully open and you need not fear killing the bees.

The quassia and soap spray is also the best pesticide for killing the caterpillars of the raspberry beetle (*Byturus tormentosus*), but sparing the bees. The adult raspberry beetles emerge from hibernation in May and feed on the blossom, and in June and July the females lay eggs in the flowers where the tiny caterpillars tunnel into the fruit. Spray the

Both ladybirds and larvae eat aphids

raspberries 10 days after they start flowering, and loganberries and boysenberries 15, and a second time 10 days later. You cannot hope to kill the beetles, for anything strong enough for this purpose will kill the bees, which are serving the useful purpose of working the blossom all the time. So make up your soap and quassia and spray with as fine a mist as possible. This will also catch the small red caterpillars of the raspberry moth (*Lampronia rubiella*) that also starts in the fruit but bores into the young shoots in April and sets them withering without fruiting.

The magpie moth, and other large non-sawfly caterpillars, need a stronger killer. One that is both strong and safe for bees, *Anthocoris* and ladybirds and larvae but not hoverfly larvae, is elder leaf wash, which is the organic gardeners' best do-it-yourself spray. Stuff about 1 pound (500 g) of elder leaves and their soft green stems into a large old saucepan with about 3½ pints (2 l) of rain water. Simmer for half an hour, topping up as the water boils away, strain (old tights are good for this), and allow to cool before spraying undiluted.

Those who make elderberry wine should 'sow' the residue as the seeds will be found to germinate like mustard and cress. Clip it for a supply of young leaves and shoots, and grow on some sturdy seedlings to keep cut back regularly like willow osier for baskets, as 'grow-it-yourself' pesticide and fungicide trees.

The American gooseberry mildew (*Sphaerotheca mors-urvae*) shows as a powdery white coating on the young shoots from April onwards, spreading fast in damp seasons, thickening to a pale brown coat that covers leaves and fruit. Start spraying at fortnightly intervals as soon as the first fruit is set. Gooseberry mildew and other bush fruit diseases are common where bushes are too closely planted, and fed with chemical nitrogen, especially blackcurrants. This also applies to caterpillars and all aphids of many species, for the higher the nitrogen level the sweeter and more attractive the sap.

There is now a biological control for all the cabbage caterpillars, a spore culture of *Bacillus thuringensis* that was once a disease of silkworms in Japan. It attacks only the cabbage white, (*Pieris brassicae*), the small white (*P. rapae*), the cabbage moth (*Mamestra brassicae*), the diamond-back moth (*Plutella xylostella*) and the tomato moth (*Lacanobia olearacea*), which is only a minor cabbage problem, but whose brown caterpillars are a curse in commercial tomato grower's houses. It is entirely specific to these species so there is no risk of it becoming a caterpillar myxomotosis and exterminating all our moths and butterflies, many of which are both harmless and beautiful. Bactospeine WP is sold in sachets, each making 8.8 pints (5 l) to spray onto the foliage the caterpillars are eating, and even if birds eat the dead caterpillars this does no harm. It is sold in boxes of ten sachets which last, if unopened, for 2-3 years.

It can be used right up to picking or harvest on any crop, and so can the modern Dutch super-soft soap, which is sufficiently powerful to kill the cabbage whitefly (*Aleyrodes proletella*). In mild winters, some adults of this increasing species come through the winter ready for a flying start. They can be laying eggs on young cabbage seedlings as early as April, and three soft soap sprayings at weekly intervals will clear them. The tiny, white moth-like adults miss most of the sprays as they rise in swarms, but direct the solution (1 part soft soap to 49 of rainwater) under the leaves where it kills the flat, scale insect-like larvae. It spares the small yellow eggs, so the later spraying clears the new generations from these.

CHAPTER 9

JUNE

Table 19: VEGETABLES FOR JUNE EATING

Available for eating	Family	Sowing	Planting
Beans, broad (longpod)	7	November	—
Beans (dried or frozen)	7	May-June	—
Beetroot	2	March	1-1
Cabbage (summer)	4	March	July
Carrots (early)	12	March	—
Kale	4	April	June-July
Lamb's lettuce	13	March	—
Landcress	4	March	—
Lettuce	3	March	—
Miner's lettuce	10	August	—
Onions (spring)	8	February	—
Peas (early)	7	—	—
Potatoes (early)	11	March-August	April-May
Radishes	4	January-May	—
Rhubarb	9	April	February
Spinach (summer)	2	February	—
Sweetcorn (frozen)	6	April-May	—
Tomatoes (bottled)	11	—	May-June

Midsummer sowings

As the year swings to the midsummer dead centre of 21 June, there is just time to fit in the final sowings of the crops that will mature for storage in the autumn, before we change over to those that grow on the 'downhill slope' of the year. The garden should be packed with food waiting for the first release of room, and the first few of anything can be eaten immature. Pick the peas hard, start the broad beans early because there will be plenty, pull carrots as small as chipolata sausages and beetroot like golf balls. Concentrate on what you like, but experiment to find what fits the changing demands of a family, for the waste of space no small garden can afford is that which grows a crop that nobody likes, after it has had a fair trial.

The first week in July is the very latest date for sowing beetroot to store, but the last in June is better, with more time to build flavour and keeping qualities. Sow the large seeds only 6 inches (15 cm) apart each way when they go in late, and there is still enough growing time to save them if the beetroot blister-fly (*Pegomyia betae*) arrives and lays eggs that become legless, white maggots, producing brown blisters as they tunnel. Pick off the attacked leaves and if more than four must be taken from one plant, give a teaspoonful of dried blood as a tonic and water it in.

The last carrots have to race to reach the 1½ inches (3.5 cm) across the top they need to be sure of keeping, so sow the maincrop not later than the last week in June, which can easily miss all carrot fly problems. Thin to 3 inches (8 cm) apart or, ideally, sow so thinly that you do not thin at all, and leave 6 inches (15 cm) between rows for this last, late sowing. Sow also the last radishes of summer as a final pair of 2-inch (5 cm) apart furrows to eat in August and on into autumn, for they will grow more slowly now the year has turned.

Windermere lettuces can still be sown for a last six-week spread of frilled and heavy heads; so can Fortune, which can go in up to mid July. The end of June should see the last picking of rhubarb, and the bed can relax and let the fruits of summer take over while it juggles with air, water and sunlight to build up its thick, black roots for forcing next spring.

The early potatoes should be flowering well, and though this is time in theory to lift them, there will be too many marble-sized tubers for economy, so wait till the petals have dropped before taking the first, thrusting the fork in well down the sides of the ridges to avoid wasting the crop by spearing, for careless forking costs spuds.

Planting the cabbage tribe

The most urgent planting, as soon as room is available, is the Autumn Spear sprouting broccoli, to crop from September on into November. Dig up the transplanted plants from the waiting bed (which can wait on into July), hold the leaves in a bunch and cut them across the top, 1 inch (2.5 cm) above the growing point in the middle. This seemingly savage treatment reduces the area through which the leaves transpire water and is a great help to plants moved when large through waiting for other crops to finish. Take out trowel holes 18 inches (45 cm) apart and 2 feet (60 cm) between rows and fill them up with water from the can, before you dig your plants. They can then go straight in after they are sliced, have the soil firmed round them and a final top watering. Winningstadt, the August-October eating cabbage, is an equally urgent candidate for the first available space.

The June and July transplanting of cabbage-tribe vegetables must often take place late and in drought, so this system works for all of them. If plants have been lost, or sowing was missed, late cabbage can be enjoyed by sowing Red Drumhead in pairs 2 feet (60 cm) apart each way and thinning to the best, for this kind puts down a taproot fast and missing the shock of transplanting allows it to catch up, though the heads may be rather smaller. It is a delicious cabbage, cooked or raw, and far too good to have its vitamins destroyed by pickling vinegar.

These winter crops all follow others that had manure and have their nitrogen for a quick start from the roots of the pea tribe. If they are overfed with either chemicals or manure they will grow soft and sappy, and fail to last the winter. This is particularly important with sprouting broccoli and the kales. As the peas finish, take out the sticks or stakes and wire, clip the haulm for compost, hoe off the surface weeds and trowel in the cabbage types, which all appreciate firm soil. The Sutton broad beans from the first sowing usually finish fast enough to fit in lettuce and radish where they came out.

Celery-planting time

Winter celery is also clamouring for

room, and there is no need to dig the slit-trench-size pits of the past. Dig in compost or manure if you have any to spare, or 4 ounces a square yard (110 g per 0.83 m²) of blood, fish and bone if not. Then take out two wide 'V's with the hoe corner 4-5 inches (10-12 cm) across and 3 inches (8 cm) deep, 2 feet (60 cm) apart, and put in the plants at 1 foot (30 cm) intervals along the bottom. Water them as a start and then give weekly waterings of comfrey liquid manure, which should now be ready from the mid May cut.

By mid August, the plants should be over 1 foot (30 cm) high, ready for any side shoots to be broken off from their bases before the modern version of 'earthing up'. The first step needs two people – one to hold the stems bunched together and the other to slip a rubber band over the top, like those used round cos lettuces such as Little Gem or Winter Density to bring them on to delicious long crispness in about four days.

Then heap soil shovelled from between the rows to fill the furrows and go about 3 inches (8 cm) up the stems – again easier with two people, one each side of the row. Three weeks later, heap leafmould or peat from both sides of the row right up to the bunched leaves at the top of the sticks to ensure freedom from frost. Whack the sides flat and firm with the spade and protect the covering from washing down with 15-inch (38 cm) squares of flat plastic, or even glass – anything that will last without rotting in the rain and store flat in the shed for use year after year. Take off the squares, spread the leafmould and dig the celery as required.

The best leafmould for this will be the mowings-hastened heap made from last autumn's leaves, which should be ready by early September. Peat is expensive, but this is a good end for a bale that has been bought and used to store root vegetables in for three years and that may now hold storage-rot spores. Celery is not a rotated crop, so it can fit wherever the right space is ready at the right time, and the ground levelled ready for the next crop which will appreciate the humus.

Organic pest and weed control in June

There will be plenty of mowings available in June and July, with ample comfrey as the bed matures. If there is a comfrey surplus beyond the need for liquid-manure production, especially when the first blossoms on the first tomato trusses are showing pea-sized fruitlets, spread some between the tomato rows and between the bush fruit. Covered down with mowings and kept well away from the stems, this will suppress weeds and make a surface compost. If the garden is troubled with a wasp nest of the type that shows as a tunnel (like a mousehole) in a bank, with such steady traffic in and out that one almost expects to see an enterprising beetle outside selling evening papers, wait till well after sunset and dump a barrowload of mowings on top. This will heat and demand oxygen, which it can take from the supply inside the wasp nest and by morning it will have killed the lot without poison or problems.

Weeds grow fast in June, and where perennials such as creeping buttercup between bush fruit are hard to dig and not easy to kill with a mowings mulch, newspapers are an answer. Save or get from neighbours any large newspapers printed on good-quality paper, for four thicknesses of each, weighed down with stones, will exclude light most effectively from June onwards. For paths, try a mixture of creosote in boiling water, in a proportion of 1-8, sprinkled on the weeds in dry weather when there will be a minimum run-off. Do not get it on your skin, or on the lawn or plants. It contains phenols which have a soil bacterium to break them down and as creosote is a product of wood distillation, it will not leave anything permanent in the path, where nothing eats. It is cheaper and more effective than a blowlamp or a flame gun, which takes a long time merely to kill off surface weeds.

The key to weedkilling by organic methods is timing. Cutting docks in the first week in June, so that they make safe compost material before the seeds ripen, and again in September, does the maximum damage to monster specimens. This also kills out ragwort. For thistles, remember the saying, 'Cut in June and cut too soon, cut in July 'tis sure to die' from the many small farmers who cleared their fields by careful cutting and the modern organic farmers who time their silage cuts to control their weeds without spreading dock seeds in the manure from the cattle that eat the silage. If large quantities of mowings can be obtained from a sports ground in June, this is the best time to pile them at least 1 foot (30 cm) deep on really bad perennial weeds such as ground elder and convolvulus. The idea is to have them thick enough to heat and mat to a solid, slimy mess which will exclude light and air at a season when the weeds need these most in their maximum growth period.

The root secretions of *Tagetes minuta*, a relative of French and African marigolds, will kill ground elder, and convolvulus less effectively, if planted 1 foot (30 cm) apart each way into weeds that have merely been cut down, though most people plant after they have cleared the bed to kill the left-in roots. Sow in March on a window-sill or in April in the open, and pot or transplant when the seedlings are about 1 foot (30 cm) high in June. They will grow to 10 feet (3 m) by October or November, producing a mass of compost material with a strong, antiseptic smell used to repel fleas in Africa, where it has run wild.

The stems can be as thick as a thumb and need bashing with an axe-back on something hard so they break down. The ground-elder roots will be found blackened and hollow from the effect of the thiophenes in the root secretions used by some plants as weapons in the underground wars they fight. However, this cannot be used to clear out ground elder and convolvulus from a border, for the roots of the weeds can hide in the herbaceous-plant clumps. The small star-like flowers of *T. minuta* in October arrive too late to set any seed in this country, so there is no risk of it becoming a worse weed than the ones it kills (as it is in Australia, where it is called 'Stinking Rogers' after the amateur gardener who let it escape).

Organic fruit care in June

June is pruning time for cherries when, in addition to the search and snip for dieback as for all stone fruit, 3 to 4 inches (8-10 cm) of each strong, young shoot can be removed, to put more strength into ripening blossom buds along the rest of the shoot for the next year and to take out the soft growth which the cherry blackfly (*Myzus cerasi*) attacks first, on the principle of pinching out the tips of broad beans to stop their blackfly. This is not very effective, because cherry shoots stay young for so much of their length and the small side shoots, which should be pinched back to two or three buds – whichever points along the wall – are equally attractive to the aphids.

One way round is to paint a grease band on the trunk, taking care to paint the wall behind it too, and a strip along the house wall to stop ants carrying up blackfly as 'house cows'. This is far more effective for bush or standard cherries which need only a dieback search and the removal of worn-out, crowding or crossing branches.

Apart from birds, defeated by nylon netting hung in front of the wall, the main loss of fruit, cherries, nectarines, peaches, plums and apricots is 'June drop' which is a natural thinning from trees in the open, but increased for wall specimens because narrow beds beside houses are often very dry. Run a hose in the bed at least once a week through June to give a real soaking, but when planting any fruit against a house wall, make sure that the soil is not heaped above the damp course in a raised bed, for repeated soakings will suck into the brickwork and mean damp stains and peeling wallpaper for the room inside. Wall fruits have relatively weak roots so do no harm by drawing water from under the foundations, but never plant a poplar, weeping willow, or anything fast-growing closer than 20 feet (6 m) from a house.

The new dwarfing stocks, Pixy for plums and Colt for cherries, save space on walls and enable these vigorous fruits to be grown where they can be protected from birds by hanging netting. Give them plenty of water but do not soak the wall.

It is possible to time spraying to catch codling moths when they are just hatched and before they are safe inside the fruit. Ingenious battery-powered light traps, whatever their colour, fail because only the male moths are fools enough to be caught before there is a population fall from too many spinsters – the surviving males just work harder.

Both sexes can be caught before they have laid their eggs with traps hung in the trees through June and July. Collect jam jars, pour about 1 inch (2.5 cm) of a mixture of one part black treacle to ten of hot water and cover these with pieces of the coarsest mesh nylon curtain net you can find, ideally 1/4 inch (6 mm), secured with rubber bands. Hang these in your trees conveniently low for refilling with a small spouted can. These will exclude bees, wasps and larger moths, which could jam the traps, but codling moths (*Cydia pomonella*), plum fruit moths (*Cydia funebrana*), small ermine moths and tortrix moths, also tiny, crawl through the meshes and cannot get out again. The proof of the experiment lies in the fall in the number of windfall apples, for where the caterpillar crawls in near the calyx it weakens the stalk as it eats, and windy nights bring the best of the ripening crop thudding down.

These often show early ripening, as they struggle to finish off their pips and attract an eater to spread their seeds, while the caterpillars hope that you will not use the organic gardener's 'secret weapon' – tidiness. Pick up your windfalls every day so that caterpillars cannot finish feeding and escape to pupate, hatch late and produce another generation in September to attack the late varieties. This picking chore is well worthwhile for those who have deep freezes, apart from the value of knowing how well (or badly) your organic pest control is working.

Cut open the apples to check how many have caterpillars, and if the entry hole has wet, red brown, tunnellings protruding, your pest is not codling moth but apple sawfly and you could catch it with quassia and soap spray. Slice up some fruit and try liquidized and eaten raw, to see how ripe looking it has to be before it is worth liquidizing and storing in small polythene bags for winter eating. Cut them up quickly so they have no time to go brown, and you will bless your own foresight when imported, organically grown apples cost the Earth. Your apples should be well-chosen flavourful varieties too good to waste in your dustbin. They may have grubs, but they are free of pesticide residues. Those who disagree are lucky

– they do not have allergies.

Caterpillars that drop mature from the fruit, or escape from windfalls, race towards the trunks of mature trees that offer safe hibernation homes in the bark crevices. The answer for these is mutton cloth. This is the loosely woven cotton material that your butcher tears off frozen mutton carcases and throws away. Ask him for some for, apart from its use in the orchard it makes excellent car polishing or hand wiping rags once it has been washed and hung out to dry. This is rather more effective than the jute sacking that was once tied round fruit trees (now replaced by paper and polythene), which past head gardeners used.

Cut lengths of the mutton cloth long enough to go round the trees with an overlap, fold it in four to make a 'belt' about 6 inches (16 cm) wide and tie it with string top and bottom about 1 foot (30 cm) above ground to be clear of weeds and grass. The caterpillars will take it for safe winter quarters, until it is removed for destruction in October and replaced with a greaseband to catch the wingless female winter-moths climbing to lay their eggs on the branches. The last of the codling moths will have gone up by then, but the mutton cloth may as well stay on to trap the apple blossom weevils (*Anthonomus pomorum*) on their way down to hibernate in dead leaves and loose litter near the trees after starting their year feeding on the blossom in the spring, pupating under the dead petals and feeding on the leaves until August.

Codling moths lay eggs from June to August on stalks and leaves where the newly hatched caterpillars have only a short journey down to the fruit. A great many climb up out of the fruit and along the relatively smooth young bark towards the crevices and rough surfaces of the main branches and trunk. It is easy to secure smaller mutton cloth

The cloth band stops codling moth caterpillars climbing up the tree in July through to October and the grease band traps wingless female winter moths as they travel down the tree trunk from October to March

bands to this younger bark with sticky tape and trap still more. Trying these measures one at a time and measuring the windfall reduction from each and together could be an interesting hobby for someone who was both retired and observant.

Vegetable pest control in June

The pea moth (*Cydia nigricans*) lays its eggs between early June and the end of August and once inside the pod the caterpillars are safe from spraying, becoming the familiar maggots found when shelling peas and a real problem for those who grow peas for drying. Spray with quassia and soft soap or elder about a week after the first flowering and again a fortnight later, to catch the caterpillars when they are crawling outside, like codling-moth caterpillars on the fruitlets.

Cutworms or surface caterpillars are active and can slaughter newly planted cabbage plants, so bring out the painted tins and stand them over the seedlings, and also over lettuce. There is a gain anyway from the effect of shelter and warmth from the sun on the black surface. Tins will also baffle slugs which will not climb vertically up a tall tin, but as this trick shades the plant if left on for a whole wet summer, it is only useful for protecting treasures for short periods.

There are many trapping methods, including putting out soup plates full of equal parts of milk and water, and clearing out the drowned slugs with a broom and refuelling; while beer, sweetened with brown sugar is a good but expensive filling for the 'slug pub', a plastic gadget that is proof against cats, hedgehogs and rain. A cheaper remedy is the old Belgian and French one of sinking a wine bottle with the neck level with the soil surface, and just half an inch or so of beer at the bottom. The slugs crawl in attracted by the scent and cannot climb out up the smooth sides. When beer traps for slugs were invented, landlords would present the contents of the drip trays free to good-customer gardeners, but today, in an ecology-minded age, they 'recycle' the froth spilled from drawing pints, and the slugs get nothing on the house.

Collecting slugs by the thousand on warm June nights (with 10-11 pm the best hunting period) is tedious, and slicing them through with a tin blade hammered sharp on the end of a broomstick is not for the squeamish, though the bodies attract other slugs so more can be massacred. Metaldehyde and other poisons also kill the hedgehogs which are the best natural controllers, and can also poison cats and dogs. Two safe substances are Fertosan slug destroyer, based on aluminium sulphate (a harmless substance also used by alpine gardeners to cancel out lime by its lock-up effect for lime-hating gentians), and a mixture of one part of alum and seven parts of slaked lime. Mix the two very thoroughly and scatter thinly on the surface on mild moist evenings.

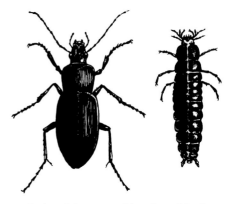

Both the violet ground beetle and its larva eat quantities of slugs' eggs

CHAPTER 10
JULY

Table 20: VEGETABLES FOR JULY EATING

Available for eating	Family	Sowing	Planting
Beans, broad (longpod)	7	November	—
Beans (dried or frozen)	7	May-June	—
Beans, French	7	May	—
Beetroot (fresh)	2	March	—
Cabbage	4	June	July
Carrots (early)	12	March	—
Cauliflowers	4	February	April
Celery	12	March-April	May-June
Kale	4	April	June-July
Kohlrabi	4	March-April	—
Lamb's lettuce	13	May	—
Landcress	4	May	—
Lettuce	3	April	—
Miner's lettuce	10	May	—
Onions (spring)	8	March	—
Peas (early)	7	February	—
Potatoes (early)	11	—	April-May
Radishes	4	March-August	—
Spinach, New Zealand	1	March	—
Spinach (summer)	2	April	—
Tomatoes (bottled)	11	—	May-June

July sees the early potatoes lifted row by row, with their haulm taken to the compost heap. Before planting anything after potatoes, dig over the bed to remove any left-in tubers, which will not only be weeds growing in the wrong place next year, but also carry the spores of potato blight, *Phytophthora infestans*.

Potato-blight problem
This shows first in cold, dull, moist weather in July as rounded dark-brown patches round the edges of the leaves which spread rapidly and blacken the whole haulm, including the stems. This reduces the food supply to the tubers so there is a tiny crop, and the spores wash down from the foliage through the soil, infecting the potatoes and causing them to rot when stored. The best preventative measure is to choose blight-resisting varieties such as Maris Peer or Wilja (second earlies), or Record, Romano,

Kerr's Pink or the new Cardinal and Cara, reputed to be the most resistant yet among the maincrops, but none are nearly 100 per cent blight-proof. Therefore, when the moist dark-brown patches show first at the tips of the leaves, spray with burgundy mixture or bordeaux mixture which can be bought ready for mixing.

If the disease continues to spread, cut down all the haulm and take it away for composting, for blight does not live long on the foliage and is killed at 120°F (50°C). Wait for three weeks before lifting the potatoes to give any spores on the surface time to die out. At intervals, pick over the small crop that remains, for blighted tubers rot and this spreads to others in contact with them.

In dull, cold summers, spray first in the last week in June, spray again three weeks later, and a third time in another three weeks. In the Midlands spray first in mid July and in the north towards the end of the month. This preventive spray will keep the blight off and is routine for commercial growers – organic and inorganic. Most gardeners trust to luck,

immune varieties and the fact that garden plots are so scattered that the disease misses many of them, though it sweeps through allotments.

The disease is far worse in tomatoes, which share membership of the order *Solanaceae* with potatoes (which catch it first). Unless July is dry and bright, spray with burgundy mixture during the first week in July in the south and early August in the north, and spray every two weeks. The spores blow from potato crops and go quite high in moist weather, so they can arrive from a distance. The disease shows as large, russet-brown, marbled areas on the green fruit and dark brown streaks on leaves and stems. There are no immune tomato varieties and if there is potato blight in your district, spray. Keep a tin of burgundy or bordeaux mixture in stock.

The tomatoes will need their side shoots removing, and tying as they grow taller, tying a first knot firmly round the stake, and then one beyond the stem where the loop can get a grip under a leaf. Tomato plants often fork about 1 foot (30 cm) from the ground and both shoots can be trained up the stake, but not more. Outdoor tomatoes can yield 8 pounds (4 kg) of fruit each, and with a variety that ripens well off the plants – like Harbinger, for bottling and deep freezing – they are a storing crop like apples, rather than a few weeks eating and then too much green fruit for chutney.

The sweetest tomato variety is Gardener's Delight, with small but tasty fruit that makes a good concentrate, liquidized uncooked for the freezer. The thin skin of Market King, the ripening of the plantability of Harbinger and the flavour of Gardener's Delight would make an ideal amateur's tomato, if only the seed companies were to consider their small customers.

Give them a weekly feed with liquid comfrey, and there is no reason why

Potato blight starts at the leaf edges

this, or seaweed foliar feed, should not be added to bordeaux or burgundy mixtures, for there is no chemical reaction between them.

Chinese radish and cabbage take-away

Midsummer Day was high noon and it is already late enough to sow the Chinese radishes and cabbages which bolt swiftly to seed if sown in the morning of the year. There are three varieties of these radishes, all excellent winter vegetables to grate raw in salads from October even to April, or to cook like turnips with a radish flavour. China Rose is the best known, red and white, like a giant French Breakfast, but up to 4 inches (10 cm) in diameter and 6 or even 8 inches (15-20 cm) long, growing up to 1½ pounds (750 g) of root from 1 foot (30 cm) of row. Sow it in July or August in 1 inch-deep (2.5 cm) furrows 8 inches (20 cm) apart, with the large seeds in pairs at 6-inch (15 cm) intervals, thinned to the best of each. They can be lifted and stored like carrots in October or left in to dig as required.

Black Spanish is also known as Bavarian because it is served raw, and sliced into sticks in beer halls, where its stronger flavour is reputed to encourage beer-drinking among the rare Bavarians who need encouragement. This is grown in exactly the same way, but it has a black skin so needs peeling rather than just scrubbing and is turnip- rather than radish-shaped. As this kind sits on the surface and can get eaten by slugs it is best dug and stored.

Japanese All-Seasons is long and pale cream, rather like a white Icicle radish but up to 1 foot (30 cm) long and 2 inches (5 cm) across the top. This does well on sandy soils for its long, tapered root will go down over 18 inches (45 cm) after moisture. Unlike the other two, it can also be sown in March or April for summer eating, scrubbed and sliced for salads or fried as 'radish chips'. It is best left in to dig as needed, because it will not keep if the long taproot is broken.

The Chinese cabbage is *Brassica pekinensis*, an entirely different species from the ancestors of our cabbage tribe, but it still gets clubroot, so should be grown in the cabbage section of the rotation. The best variety is Pei Tsai, which looks like a pale-green cos lettuce, about 15 inches (38 cm) high. Greengrocers are now selling it as 'Chinese leaves' for salads. From July sowings it will be ready from September on into autumn, finishing in the hard frosts of November.

Sow the large seeds like the radishes, but 8 inches (20 cm) apart in the rows. Neither the cabbages nor the radishes cross with our familiar varieties and seed is easily saved by sowing when the day length is *increasing*, letting the pods ripen and split before putting them in chitting trays to dry.

Chinese cabbage has always been handicapped by sowing at the wrong season and cooking the wrong way. Unlike our cabbage tribe, the Chinese species contains no sulphur, so produces no smell when cooking, and those who are allergic to the cabbage race should try if they can eat it safely. There is a new variety, Sanpan, which can be sown in April to enjoy in summer, but this is an F_1 hybrid, so seed cannot be saved. A modernized Chinese recipe is to slice the cabbage lengthways and then crossways, after removing the outer leaves. Heat some soya or corn oil in a frying pan and drop in a quarter cabbage which will exude enough juice to make water unnecessary, and then drop in the rest. Simmer in its own juice for about eight minutes and serve with the distinctive flavour that made it 'sell like hot cabbages' in China to the tea-clipper Captains who brought them to

England in the 1840s.

Swedes and turnips are better sown now for winter storage, after an earlier sowing at the end of March for those who like them from May onwards. They are tastier grown fast to tennis-ball size than the heavy cannon balls greengrocers crash into the scales. Sow in ½-inch (1 cm) deep furrows 8 inches (20 cm) apart and thin to 8 inches (20 cm) between plants. Those who like turnip leaves as a green vegetable can pick from their plants after these have been sown four weeks (without robbing the same specimens each time), as though they were winter spinach, and still enjoy their roots without loss of quality, but losing some yield.

It is the season for sowing the hardy winter salads so that they can get their roots spread and their foliage up and give them time to regrow from an October cut. Miner's lettuce, or winter purslane, can be cut from under snow, but it will not put on much growth in December and January, any more than savoy cabbages or Brussels sprouts do. If there is space to spare in July or August, sow it thinly in rows, ideally 1 foot (30 cm) apart to allow room to snip the clumps with large scissors without treading on them. You need as many rows as you can spare room for, as they will still be growing in late spring when salads are short.

Landcress should go in now too, sown the same way – valued for its strong sharp taste and its high content of vitamins A and C. If you have enough, it can be liquidized and used as the base for sauces at a time when parsley and mint have little flavour. Do not forget a final sowing of Little Gem and Windermere lettuces and take advantage of the autumn warmth that is still in the soil to grow a last crop and ensure that you do not eat the winter varieties. The aim of organic gardening is to grow more healthy food and salads all the year round, to provide the green leaf vitamins, folic and pantothenic acids, catalase, the enzyme from raw vegetables and the fibre that we all need.

Leeks and onions

Gardeners today rarely have room to grow the leeks like bolsters that won prizes as forgotten flower shows. July planting after early potatoes brings 2-inch (5 cm) thick stems, while if they wait till August they will be only as fat as candles, but just as good if you only have room to spare then. Make holes 8 inches (20 cm) apart along a garden line, with a long dibber (use an old spade or fork handle with the end re-pointed; or an edging tool with the blade broken off, which gives a nice steel-shod tip). Drop a leek plant, roots first, down each hole, fill this with water, move the line 8 inches (20 cm) and plant another row. Teach your family to enjoy leeks, for these have no clubroot and are perhaps our easiest winter vegetable.

Onions from sets, and the Japanese autumn-sown variety Express Yellow, will be ready well ahead of the spring-sown varieties, and their leaf tips yellow in July, ready to be bent over at rather more than a right-angle to the ground so the necks break and they begin to ripen. Leave them ten days to dry, and dig them up to lie in the ever-useful tomato or grape trays; stack these one on top of each other in a shed at night or during wet weather and put out in the sun. These fast onions not only leave room earlier for a wider choice of crops to follow them, but give a better chance of getting good weather for drying the bulbs thoroughly.

Wring off the onion tops for burning or dustbin dumping because of the risk of a late compost heap failing to heat sufficiently to kill fungus spores, and drop the bulbs down the legs of lad-

Above left Bury crushed or uncrushed brassica stumps with kitchen wastes in winter-dug trenches for runner beans sown in May. These decay to humus with the help of the bacteria in the bean roots.

Above right In addition to a good bean crop and the humus, this 'composts' the eggs of the mealy cabbage aphid and hibernating cabbage white fly, gaining poisonless pest control as well as fertility.

Below left Melt holes with a candle in the bottoms of yogurt cartons, and fit these over the roots of brassica plants so cabbage root flies cannot lay eggs where the stem meets the soil.

Below right Sowing sweetcorn through discarded polytunnel plastic germinates weeds but stops them seeding. Fasten the plastic down with stakes to hold down thrusting weeds and clear for compost after harvest, gaining fewer weeds next season.

Above Surface caterpillars eat cabbage plants and other soft seedlings at ground level. Protect these with bottomless and topless tins. Paint them with black bitumen paint to protect them from rust and to give your seedlings a sunnier warmed start.

Below Egg-loaded carrot flies fly low, and an 18-inch (46 cm) high barrier of clear polythene or papronet defeats them completely. The protection from the anti-fly barrier gives a better carrot crop as 'spin-off'.

Above Fit tins over round stake ends and hammer the tins full of nail holes. Fill them with potato peelings and bury them at ground level to trap the black millepedes that eat holes in bulbs and tubers.

Below Growing alternate rows of carrots and onions to baffle carrot flies with onion scent only works with distant flies. Those from next door just use their eyes.

dered tights – the more ladders the better because this improves the ventilation through the nylon. Open-weave or 'fishnet' stockings were best, but these are no longer readily available, and tights offer a pair of onion-storing containers to hang by their middles in a dry attic. Attics can get very hot in the warm days of spring and it is worth re-sorting the onions into greengrocer's nets as used for pumpkins, removing any that have gone soft, and hanging them in a cooler place, for after April the problem is to stop them sprouting.

Organic pest control in July

Look along your lettuce rows for any plants flopping suddenly. Dig these up and you will find yellow or grey aphids eating the roots. These are the lettuce root aphids (*Pemphigus bursarius*) which spend most of the year on poplar trees, but spend summer holidays on sow thistle and lettuce roots. Water the rows with cigarette-end nicotine, allowing seventy-two hours before eating the lettuces.

There is an excellent biological control for the greenhouse whitefly (*Trialeurodes vaporariorum*) – the tiny wasp *Encarsia formosa*. But, the smallest quantity of parasitized larvae that it pays the breeders to send, is enough to treat **400** square feet (37 m²) of greenhouse space. This is expensive for small greenhouses. Many years ago, the HDRA, with the co-operation of members of The Fuchsia Society, tested the idea that growing French marigolds in the greenhouse will repel whitefly – for this pest attacks fuchsias as well as several other greenhouse plants. They used potted bedding French marigolds which make good pot plants, and had no more trouble. Other gardeners have been successful planting *Tagetes patula* hybrids between their tomatoes. The most certain method though is to use soft soap, using the Dutch brand (the British is cheaper and good enough for aphids) because the eggs are tougher, and you will need several sprayings, spraying well under the leaves. This is also effective against scale insects and mealy bugs (*Pseudococcus obscurus*) which can also be pests of houseplants. Wash your tomatoes well before eating – they may taste soapy otherwise.

Summer pruning and pest control

Hard pruning in winter makes apples and pears grow more wood, because the roots have less growth to support, which is why sawing branches out of an elderly tree (especially if some are cankered) can give it new vigour. Summer pruning in July 'slims' trees growing too big for small gardens by reducing the carbohydrate intake from the sunlight on the living leaves, and so cutting down their calories.

Shorten the leaders by a quarter of their length and the side shoots by two

Where to prune apples in summer

thirds. The prunings are soft in July and can go straight on the compost heap. The effect is to put more strength into ripening fruit buds rather than growing more wood. It has also put your tree 'on a diet' and reduced its growth speed, which is important if it was grafted on an ordinary crab-apple stock and not one of the new dwarfing varieties.

At winter pruning time reduce the leaders so they are left with a third of their first length, and their lesser contemporaries to three or four buds – whichever points away from the centre of the tree. This is exactly the pruning recommended for February – the difference is that you have gone over the tree quickly in summer first to have fewer leaves working, and gained better ripening of fruiting buds.

In late July, the summer pruning of cordon apples and pears consists of snipping back any new, young shoots from the main stem to three leaves and any from the existing shoots to a single leaf. Horizontally trained trees should have their side shoots shortened to

three leaves each. Both types of trained tree are pruned hard because, like wall peaches, cherries and plums, they are grown intensively in little space.

The June drop is now over and it is time for the final thinning of peaches, nectarines and apricots. When the fruitlets are the size of thumbnails, thin to 8 inches (20 cm) between them. This is approximate, for if you have a strong branch with only about seven fruit on it, all crowded up one end, leave them all on even if they are only 4 inches (10 cm) apart, which just stops them touching each other. It also pays to thin Kirke's Blue, the rare flavour plum that does well on walls.

A taste for Coxes

Today the public demands Coxes all the year round (as though they were a favourite brand of fish fingers) and the growers and wholesalers do their best to meet this demand. The blossom is sprayed to make it set in orchards made bee-less by pesticides and sprayed again with etherol to hasten its ripening to make it available before Beauty of Bath is finished. Once, ripening an orchard of Coxes was an art. The mowings of grazing of the grassed down orchard were timed so the grass took up the excess nitrogen at the end of the summer, giving keeping quality, and the colours were described in 1920 as 'golden yellow, flushed brownish red with faint stripes and slightly russeted, with crisp yellow flesh, sweet, subacid and aromatic' by George Bunyard, the father of modern English fruit growing.

Today Coxes can be too green, too sweet and too white because the grower has now no need to worry about holding down the nitrogen by excluding pigs from the orchard to maintain keeping qualities. The whole crop is going straight into cold storage to come out as the market will take them, and he can pile on the chemical nitrogen to in-

Prune leader branches by a third and side shoots to third bud up from the main stem to restrict apple growth in winter

CORDON – AT SUMMER PRUNING
Summer pruning slows growth and increases the crop

crease the yield. Those who have only eaten Coxes straight from cold store through the supermarket, have no idea what they are missing by the loss of the room over the stables where the fruit matured on racks at a temperature of 35°F (no Celsius for Coxes) and the humidity provided by the breath of the horses below. When you bring your beautifully packed and graded Coxes home, set them out in grape or tomato trays under the bed and keep them there for at least a couple of weeks to ripen slowly. The way to enjoy tastier bought apples is to buy your own horse or buy from a good organic grower or become one yourself.

When your trees are established (about four years after planting), sow a grass seed mixture that includes wild white clover (farm seedsmen supply orchard sowing mixtures) and lime ev-

ery spring as recommended to encourage worms. The clover provides all the nitrogen needed by the trees as they like it. Mow it with a rotary or rough grass mower, whenever the grass reaches a height of 4 inches (10 cm) and let the mowings lie with lime enough to keep them at pH7.0 as this will keep the clover, the worms and the trees happy. Make the last mowing in the first or second week in July to let the grass run ahead and take up the nitrogen to ripen any of the aromatic apples related to Coxes, of which there are now many. Their flavour is due to what are called 'esters', and all are improved by 'under-bed ripening' between coldstore and consumer. If periodicals had fruit as well as wine correspondents we should be healthier people, with more civilized desserts instead of mere 'sweets'.

CHAPTER 11
AUGUST

Table 21: VEGETABLES FOR AUGUST EATING

Available for eating	Family	Sowing	Planting
Beans, broad (Windsor)	7	May	—
Beans, French	7	May	—
Beans, runner	7	—	May
Beetroot (fresh)	2	March	—
Cabbage	4	June	July
Carrots (early)	12	March	—
Carrots (Shorthorn)	12	March	—
Cauliflowers	4	February	April
Celery	12	March-April	May-June
Cucumbers (outdoors)	5	April	—
Kale	4	April	June-July
Kohlrabi	4	April-May	—
Lamb's lettuce	13	May	—
Landcress	4	May	—
Lettuce	3	April	—
Marrows; Courgettes	5	April	—
Miner's lettuce	10	May	—
Onions	8	March	—
Onions (spring)	8	March	—
Peas (maincrop)	7	April	—
Potatoes (early)	11	—	March
Radishes	4	March-August	—
Spinach, New Zealand	1	March	—
Spinach (summer)	2	April	—
Sweetcorn	6	April-May	—
Tomatoes (outdoor)	11	—	May

August sowing for winter and spring
There are still weeks of growing weather left and time to sow the winter and spring leaf crops in two stages – one now and one in September. Lifting the onions early, with even the sown crop finished by the end of the month, re-leases more ground, and there is space between the wide-spaced cabbage tribe for sowing landcress, lamb's lettuce and miner's lettuce. The August sowings, which will be eaten before the later crops like broccoli, kale and January King cabbages, can well go between

them without the risk of being trampled in the snow or when driving in stakes. Sprouting broccoli, kale and Brussels sprouts are tall and have a considerable sail area in autumn gales, so short, strong stakes to reach about 1 foot (30 cm) out of the ground, driven in on the side of the stems away from the prevailing wind and tied firmly with good string, will save root breakages.

Autumn-sown onions do not need firm soil because by the time they want something to push against, the ground will have firmed in ten months without digging. Organic fertilizers or even compost should not be dug in either, for winter crops can suffer in hard winters if they have too much nitrogen. They will do very well on what they gather from the autumn and late-summer peak of bacterial activity that is usually snatched by chickweed. Compost and rotted manure dug under in autumn is for ground that is to be sown with green manure crops in September or October.

White Lisbon onions can be sown as August ends or September begins, in ½-inch (1 cm) deep furrows 8 inches (20 cm) apart on ground raked level and smooth, aiming at 1 inch (2.5 cm) between seeds. Those who are really fond of spring onions can sow single or even half rows in early March, in April and May.

Onion varieties for autumn sowing can be sown in the same way, but thinned to 6 inches (15 cm) apart, and the thinnings eaten as 'spring onions'. There is a risk in growing them too large from earlier sowings so they run to seed, but in Scotland and the north, early August is not too soon if they are to be growing well before winter. They will be helped by feeding with comfrey liquid manure in March and April.

Winter lettuces can be sown from early August in rows 1 foot (30 cm) apart and thinned to this much between them as September ends, because if they do not touch each other they are safer from slugs. Winter Density, the hardiest cos, can go closer and so can the old Arctic King, about 8 inches (20 cm) each way, but Imperial Winter or Valdor, larger and newer kinds, need the wider spacing. The thinnings can be transplanted onto a sunny bed, between tomatoes, if the final pickings can be made carefully, and the plants taken up without treading on the lettuce crop, to heart up in spring. Hoe off the weeds and taken them away, for slugs are designed to clean up decaying vegetable wastes – and lettuces too, so the less food left for them on the surface in winter the better. September sowings care late to transplant, but these too can be made between tomato rows, with the protection of wire pea-guards – not against birds, but careless feet.

Lettuce is non-rotational and can fit anywhere that has time to let the spring-hearting crop finish, and it fits well on the sunny bed on a south-facing slope that rotates tomatoes, drying beans, and pumpkins and cucumbers. The spinach tribe is also non-rotational, and can follow lettuce or drying beans, sown in August or September between the rows after merely hoeing, although caution is needed at harvest and clearing. Nothing can be sown between pumpkins or cucumbers, so the border can rest after digging, composting and manuring.

Sow broad-leafed prickly spinach (it has prickly *seeds*, not leaves – unlike the round-seeded summer varieties) in clusters 8 inches (20 cm) apart, and 15 inches (38 cm) between rows, to allow room to walk between them for picking. Perpetual spinach sown in the same way has rather lower oxalic acid and stands longer into the spring, but Swiss or Ruby chard is by far the most rewarding of this group of winter crops. Space it 18 inches (45 cm) between the rows to allow the big leaves to be twisted off more easily. Sow sufficient of them that there is no need to pick any too hard, and give them time to grow and stand the winter, always where the previous crop had the manure.

August fruit harvest

August is traditionally a month for holidays, but leaving a garden full of food should make it easier to find a neighbour to water, trim tomato plants, and pick fruit, in return for a share of the produce. The September routine will be much the same, and a policy of 'You look after my garden and I look after yours,' could well be arranged between organic gardening neighbours.

Make aprons with pockets to hold large jars (like the now scarce Kilners) and pick with both hands direct into these and tip them into plastic containers or bags when they are full and these can then go into the freezer within an hour. Soft fruit starts losing vitamin C as soon as it is picked, and it is also destroyed by light, so it is the darkness in the freezer that is as important as the saving of time in dealing with the blackcurrant crop. It was found also that cutting the three-to-four day gap between field and kitchen via market, wholesaler and greengrocer to a few hours, and storage in darkness showed

twice as much vitamin C in blackcurrants bottled six months earlier, than in a sample bought 'fresh' in London. Vitamin C varies according to the variety and Table 22 shows the average content, picked over a seven-day period at Long Ashton Research Station in a trial with fruit taken direct to the laboratory to give accurate analysis.

The fruit really worth making jam with are strawberries, for these neither freeze nor bottle well, and their delicious flavour justifies the quantity of white sugar that jam making adds to our diets. Blackcurrants and raspberries are better value bottled without any sugar at all. All fruit is designed to be eaten at peak ripeness when its vitamins and flavour are at their best, and its seeds in ideal condition for natural sowing. When we eat carrots we are (from the viewpoint of the carrot) stealing the hoarded food that should have thrust up a tall seed head to toss its personal harvest high and wide upon the wind. Fruit 'wants' to be eaten, providing colour contrast to draw the flying customers and taste to build up the brand 'loyalty' that will bring the same customers year after year to spread the seeds in their bodies as effectively as blackberries, briars and hawthorns are sown on almost every ungrazed acre.

As the cost of even pick-it-yourself

TABLE 22: AVERAGE VITAMIN C CONTENT OF BLACKCURRANTS ACCORDING TO VARIETY

	Vitamin C Mg per 100g
Baldwin	242
Seabrook's Black	205
Wellington's XXX	204
Davidson's Eight	203
Westwick Choice	235
Boskoop Giant	198
Mendip Cross	196

soft fruit soars like the price of petrol to reach it, soft fruit becomes a better and better bargain in every garden. The cheapest counter-measure against the birds, which are the bushes' favourite customers, is a temporary fruit cage. Make tripods with 6-foot (2 m) bamboo canes tied firmly about 2 inches (5 cm) from the top with a 'wigwam' effect and cap each with a jam jar. These serve to support nylon netting draped generously over them sliding on their smoothness without tearing and leave room to get inside for picking. A metal fruit cage with doors is of course better, but with care to redrape the net side after every picking, the bamboo and jar system saves money and can be stored bundled and labelled until next summer. (It is important to know which net fits where when they are wanted again.)

Vegetables for the freezer

Those who are 'digging for a diet' need all the freezer space they can afford, for the electricity they use is a minor cost compared with that of solving the problems of acquiring organically grown food urgently. Treasure the space and store all you can indoors, in sheds or in the ground. Sweet corn cobs are worth freezing and tomato purée, including even those tomatoes that are cracked or split, can save space by squashing the purée into square cartons before freezing, so they fit together as 'cubes' of food rather than space wasting pillow shapes.

The test for ripeness in sweetcorn is to feel if the cobs are plump and firm and the silky tassel beyond the green sheath is withering and turning brown. Then turn back the sheath, remove a grain and press it with a thumbnail – the juice should come out rather like Devonshire cream. Do *not* wait till the grains are hard, or you will have wasted time and space on growing expensive chicken food. After a few tries the state

of the tassel tells the ripeness and readiness for freezing as well as eating freely from now until the frosts.

Tomatoes too will be ripening and it pays to pick at the light-red stage rather than wait until they are rich red and the birds attack. Blackbirds are especially fond of tomatoes and though a bamboo-tripod fruit cage can give complete protection, this makes spraying, trimming, tying and watering awkward, so pick less ripe to keep the birds waiting for real-red ripeness, while your fruit finishes safely indoors.

Cut out the canes

As each raspberry variety finishes, cut out the canes that have fruited, snipping with the points to take them off a bit *below* ground level to leave no hollow stumps where the cocoons of raspberry moth can hide. This gets rid of the raspberry aphid (*Amphorophora idaei*) that carries raspberry virus, and lets in the sun to ripen the young canes that grow well ready for their autumn pruning. Burn the canes because they can hold spores of raspberry rust and cane blight as well as aphid eggs.

The virus symptoms look very like those of the far more common problem of magnesium deficiency, with the older leaves turning yellow while the veins stay green in summer rather than changing colour as they would normally as they get ready to fall. This, however, affects large areas of the bed at once. If only a few scattered plants have it, dig them out before the aphids spread the virus further, from where the winged stage of the aphid has brought it from wild blackberries or unlucky neighbours. Before you dig up *anything* you think could have a virus, spray it thoroughly with a seaweed extract. This will show up a deficiency of one or other of the full house of trace elements that there are in seaweed by the fact that the plant will recover. If it does not recover you can fairly safely assume that it has a virus. This is a test rather than a 'cure' for the effect is only temporary.

Scatter 1 pound of dolomite per square yard (453 g per 0.84 m²) between the rows in the autumn. Dolomite is slow-acting and lasts several years, even on sandy soil where minerals run out quickest. The following May water 1 ounce (28 g) of Epsom salts (magnesium sulphate) mixed with 2 gallons (9 l) of water in a watering can along 12 feet (3.6 m) of row, as an immediate answer.

Boysenberries (a cross between a blackberry and a loganberry, larger and tastier than either) of which the thornless variety is a pleasure to prune, and the loganberries, of which the thornless variety is less sharp in taste, should also have their fruited canes cut out to leave room for the young shoots that will fruit the following year to be tied in loosely to wait for pruning in October. Blackberries fruit later, on both the old and young wood, so should wait till December.

Pest control by pruning

In August look for American gooseberry mildew (*Sphaerotheca morsuvae*), which is a white fungus on leaves, stems and berries that later turns brown. Cut off the shoot tips in August with about 4 inches (10 cm) of stem, because this is where the spores that spread the disease concentrate. Then spray the bushes with ½ pound (220 g) of soft soap and 1 pound (450 g) of ordinary washing soda, in 5 gallons (22 l) of cold water. Spray again in the spring when they start to flower and again when the fruit is well set. This fungicide, which is weaker than lime-sulphur, spares *Anthocoris*, does not harm varieties that are 'sulphur shy' (few gardeners know their older gooseberries by name), and serves also for the less-common European gooseberry mildew (*Microsphaera*

grossulariae). This is thin and scanty, stays white and is mainly on the leaves, unlike the American species which is chiefly on stems and berries. Try the 1-3 strength urine on this one, because it is a powdery mildew on the surface.

Red and white currants, unlike black, fruit on the old wood as apples do, and can therefore be trained as cordons or fans against house or shed walls, growing in narrow beds where they can be easily protected from birds by a hanging nylon curtain. Summer prune these by pinching out the tips of new side shoots in August to strengthen the fruiting buds round their bases. After the leaves fall, shorten these shoots to 1 inch (2.5 cm), and new growth on leaders – reaching up the wall or across it – by a third of their length.

Blackcurrants are pruned in November, but look over the bushes in August (also red and white currants when summer pruning) for shoots with withered leaves or leaves and fruit dwarfed. Cut these out for burning, snipping again if there is a tunnel inside, and go on snipping till the wood is clean and white. This is caused by the creamy-white caterpillar, with black spots and a brown head, of the currant clearwing moth (*Aegeria tipuliformis*), eating away safe from spraying inside the branches,

STRAWBERRY PLANTING
Plant strawberries in August to fruit next year

which can be a serious problem if it gets established in a garden.

Start strawberry beds in August

August is the best month for starting a strawberry bed, for if they go in now or in September there is a good chance of a crop next year. Organic gardeners rotate their strawberry beds like other crops, partly as a disease-control measure and partly to use the humus from the bed through the vegetable garden. The principle is to plant each year at the end of the rotation beds, and start another each year, using either bought plants or runners from your own bed, so that there are four – one at each stage, from freshly planted to four years old, and with a falling yield. Dig the oldest one up, and replant at the other end of the same bed, then dig over the old site ready to go under vegetables.

This method has the disadvantage of having four small strawberry beds instead of a single large one, but it is rather easier to surround four beds with low wire netting on short stakes that can be moved to second ends in turn, and cover each with a net that is small enough to roll up for picking, weeding or spraying, than to bend double under a large, low construction. Alternatively, have five beds, each in turn under four years' strawberries, though this means clearing a whole bed in August or September and a dip in yield. Six plots would be better: a good long rotation and a spare bed for extra crops.

Start each strawberry square with a good barrow-load of compost or well-rotted manure to 4 square yards (3.3 m²) and 3 pounds (1.3 kg) of fine bonemeal, dug in with the manure tucked well down in the trenches. Strawberries are phosphorus hungry and on poor sandy soils an extra 8 ounces a square yard (225 g per 0.83 m²)of rock phosphate is an advantage. Veganic gardeners, or vegetarians who object to bonemeal, can double the rock phosphate instead.

Royal Sovereign is still the finest early variety for flavour, but Cambridge Rival has large fruit on erect stems clear of the ground for wet seasons and resistance to redcore disease, as well as a flavour not perfect but good. Follow it with Talisman, upright and disease resisting and cropping over a long period; Redgauntlet, another heavy-cropping disease beater; and Cambridge Late Pine, to pick on into August with a delicious, almost a pineapple flavour and resistance to both mildew and frost.

Break up the clods, tread firm and rake level before planting in rows 18 inches (45 cm) apart and 1 foot (30 cm) between plants, with 1 foot (30 cm) between the last row and the wire netting at the sides of the bed. Take out trowel holes 4 inches (10 cm) wide but shallower in the middle and set each rooted runner on top of this mound with its roots spread downwards; heap the soil over them, firming it back with the handle of the trowel. Strawberries are shallow rooting and need to have their roots spread wide and their growing points or 'crowns' on the surface. If they are all bunched into a dibber hole, frost can heave them right out of the ground and they start with a handicap. Pot-grown plants should be put without breaking the soil ball, but the crown level with the soil surface.

Hoe between the rows if the weeds grow fast in a mild autumn and again in April before spreading a 2-inch (5 cm) thick mulch of peat or leafmould to hold down annual weeds. One of the 'hastened' leafmoulds will do, but not compost or mowings, because it is important not to use anything that attracts slugs. Straw, renewed each spring, is unattractive to slugs, but it is increasingly hard to get, for no organic farmer will sell what he needs for his land. Any other straw will have had a selective killer used on it, but MCPA, used in the spring of the year before harvest and spread the next spring, is allowed by the British Organic Standards as safe. It is also possible to buy ready-made strawberry mats which fit round the plants – these are excellent but prove more expensive.

As the young plants start to grow they will produce early flowers which should be nipped out to put more strength into later blossom and any stray runners should be removed. After the first spray with nicotine in April, spray with derris because you will be picking and eating the fruit. Mildew and grey mould are problems in some gardens, and dusting with flowers of sulphur is an answer. Where it is really bad, as it may be on cold, damp clays, grow Redgauntlet, which resists both. It has only a 'fair' flavour, but even that is better than no strawberries.

In the past it was usual to burn the straw and the leaves off the bed to get rid of disease and pest eggs, but the modern garden method is to clip the rows with shears at the end of the season, and take the clippings with the partly rotted straw to the compost heap. In the spring scatter 4 ounces a square yard (115 g per 0.83 m^2) of fine bonemeal (or dried sewage sludge if you can get it), and renew the peat or leafmould mulch, which will mainly have been taken under by the worms.

By the time each bed becomes ready to return to vegetable growing, it will be rich and productive with the unexpended portion of the year's rations from every season. This makes the six-bed rotation a permanent soil-enrichment programme, and suggests that on the four-bed system there should be four strawberry places on each.

CHAPTER 12
SEPTEMBER

Prepare the vegetable store
There is no need to wait for the haulm to die down on the second early potatoes, for as soon as it starts to yellow it has ceased to fatten the tubers. Dig them with care and spread them on opened-out polythene bags to dry in the sun for forty-eight hours, then pick out the reproachful fork-speared accidents for immediate eating and store the rest in paper sacks that are all we can buy or beg today. Think ahead to where the roots are going to go this year. It must be rat-proof, which rules out small-scale potato or root clamps outside, dark, and hold a temperature of about 35°F (2°C). These are exactly the conditions offered by the wine and other cellars under the large houses of the past. New houses today sit on thin concrete rafts, and it would be easy enough while the excavating machinery is there to scoop out a cellar and build something dark, cool and convenient for the kitchen.

Lining a shed with hardboard and fibreglass is a good investment, for deep freezes also cost time and fuel to prepare and blanch the roots that could store just as easily in tea-chests, with peat, fine ashes or sand to take care of the humidity. These can be covered with old blankets as light excluders if you use the easiest trick of all – a bayonet-type light socket on the wall, not only to switch on by the door to find the vegetables you need, but to take higher wattage bulbs (up to 250), or infra-red heater bulbs, for hard winters.

Heat insulation is valuable for keep-ing stored roots (and fruit) *cool* as well as frost-free. Place a thermometer to indicate maximum and minimum temperatures in your possible storage places as well as a hygrometer, which measures humidity. Both are useful tools for any gardener because it is useless growing good food only to waste it in storage. Potatoes and roots need 34-40°F (2-5°C and 90-95 per cent humidity; apples and pears need the same temperature range but 80-90 per cent humidity. This can be provided by saucers of water, as necessary, in an attic. Onions and garlic need to be cool and dry, 35-40°F (2-5°C) and 60-70 per cent humidity, which is attic temperature without saucers, or an un-heated boxroom, while pumpkins and ripening green tomatoes need 50-60°F (10-15°C) and 60-70 per cent humid-ity. Move the max-min thermometer and hygrometer about to find the right conditions in all the places where you could fit fruit and vegetables without domestic disturbance, so you know where everything can go *before* it is time to harvest the crops.

The value of August and September room lies in there being still time for sowing with enough of the ebbing growth tide left for winter crops to succeed. Many gardeners concentrate on early and second early potatoes, with only a few Desirée, Record and Arran Consul maincrops that are dug in Octo-ber, too late to sow anything but broad beans to follow them. There is still time for winter lettuce, spring onions and the other salad crops that provide a

Table 23: VEGETABLES FOR SEPTEMBER EATING

Available for eating	Family	Sowing	Planting
Beans (dried or frozen)	7	May-June	—
Beans, French	7	May	—
Beans, runner	7	—	May
Beetroot (fresh)	2	March	—
Cabbage	4	June	July
Carrots (summer)	12	March	—
Carrots (Shorthorn)	12	March	—
Cauliflowers	4	February	April
Cucumbers (outdoor)	5	April	—
Kale	4	April	June-July
Kohlrabi	4	March-April	—
Lamb's lettuce	13	May	—
Landcress	4	May	—
Leeks	8	April	July
Lettuce	3	May	—
Marrows, courgettes	5	April	—
Miner's lettuce	10	May	—
Onions	8	March	—
Onions (spring)	8	August	—
Peas (maincrop)	7	April	—
Potatoes (second early)	11	—	March
Pumpkins	5	April	May
Radishes	4	March-August	—
Spinach, New Zealand	1	March	—
Spinach (summer)	2	April	—
Sweetcorn (fresh)	6	April-May	—
Tomatoes (outdoor)	11	—	May

change for everyone and keep up the essential food supply for those on rotating allergy diets.

Sow green manure crops in September

Growing time is important for green manure crops, which are among the organic gardener's method of conserving fertility and adding nitrogen and humus to the soil. The only time small gardens have for growing green manure crops is in winter when spare space that would otherwise grow weeds can grow fertility instead. Weeds, especially chickweed, can gather the last nitrogen of summer with other plant foods that winter rains wash away, but they cannot compete with farm crops bred to grow bulk fast for winter and early-spring grazing. There is also the important *garden* difference between crops and weeds. Most weeds have seeds that germinate over a period, with only a varied percentage coming up the first year however suitable the conditions, while others germinate at intervals like time bombs, so 'one year's weed – seven year's seed', the old gardener's saying, is quite literally true. Farm and garden varieties have had this ability bred out of them by selection through the centuries.

Perhaps the best plant-food holder for any soil is Hungarian grazing rye (not annual rye *grass* which is slower and less effective). This will grow about 15 inches (38 cm) tall from a late August or September sowing and 8 inches (20 cm) from mid October, so it can still go in after maincrop potatoes. It offers not only a bulk of leaf to dig in, but a web of root hairs so thick that it is said that if all were joined together they would reach half a mile, as extra humus rapidly available for bacterial breakdown in spring.

Dig over the cleared ground, rake it fine and level and sow at the rate of 1 ounce a square yard (28 g per 0.83 m^2) like a very thin lawn. Another method that makes seeds go further is to take out 1 inch-deep (2.5 cm) furrows with the hoe corner, 4 inches (10 cm) apart and space the seeds along them at roughly 3-inch (8 cm) intervals, covering them afterwards with the hoe. A single-furrow, hand seed-drill, ideally second-hand and shared between neighbours, saves far more time than most garden gadgets and is a more useful buy for an organic gardener's group or club than a far more costly compost chopper.

Dig in the rye before April ends, for if it grows on to tall green straw, the bacteria that decay it will increase so fast that they rob the next sown crops of nitrogen and phosphorus. Grazing rye, cut at the sappy, high-protein stage that farmers need it for stock, can be followed by potatoes or any other garden crop. Those who keep a goat can tether it on the rye and gain an increased milk yield and a happy goat (but less leaf), while still keeping the surface 'turf' and all the roots. Chickens will not eat rye.

However, rye merely holds on to the nitrogen that is already in the soil.

Winter tares are pea-tribe plants which gather nitrogen from the air and add it to the soil. Sow these from August till the first week in October, in furrows like the rye and at the same spacing; as the seed is larger, 1 ounce (28 g) sows 80 feet (24 m) of row. This sowing will be ready to turn under in March or April, when, if the soil is poor and space can be spared, another sowing can be made to dig in when the buds first show in July. Unlike rye, winter tares are attractive to chickens whose instinct tells them that they do not have the bacteria to digest cellulose like goats and cattle so must have protein and carbohydrate. Birds, moved round the garden in an ark clearing weeds, can feed off tares and save their owner the job of turning the foliage under. The fibre the chickens do not digest will have gone back in their droppings to help the humus supply.

Undersown lawns beat birds

The September sowing of winter tares offers a way of starting a new lawn where the soil is poor and the sparrows are fierce. Leave the crop until May or June when it will be in full flower, and then scatter your grass seed over the foliage. Brush and shake the foliage to make sure that all the grass seed reaches the ground. When you can see the grass is well up, set the mower as high as it will go and mow off the tares for compost material. This releases the hoarded nitrogen from them at grass-roots level and thickens up the new grass into a turf ready for autumn mowing. The tares are biennial and so die off when their job is done.

The best real clover for gardeners is the old Essex Red variety, *Trifolium pratense*, once sown with turnips after harvest on the stubble for sheep feed in spring on the South Downs of Sussex. It is cheaper than most green manures because the seeds are so tiny that 1 ounce (28 g) sows 10 square yards (8.3 m²). This is why, though the Royal Horticultural Society has recommended it as a green manure since the 1900s, it is almost unknown to modern gardeners. The problem of sowing so little is solved by mixing each ounce (28 g) thoroughly with ½ pound (225 g) of bonemeal and sowing the mixture on 4 square yards (3.3 m²). The cream-coloured bonemeal against the dark soil shows clearly where you have been, and gives a 2 ounces a square yard (55 g per 0.83 m²) dressing of organic phosphates and nitrogen to start the crop on a poor soil.

Green manure and poultry

Sow the clover on well-raked and levelled soil in August or September, ready to dig under in April when it will be up to 1 foot (30 cm) high, which was when the sheep were folded on it. It is even better for starting a lawn under than tares, with the grass seed sown in April on top of the budding clover, which of course protects the seed from birds. It it does seed itself the seedlings are killed out by mowing, unlike the perennial white clover of most lawns.

The September mowing is much appreciated by chickens, and if the ark is moved every other day so the birds do not peck it too hard it will last from early April till June, with eggs as the 'spin off' from building fertility. For green manures build fertility, while compost-material crops, like those from weeds on waste land, or sunflowers sown after dug-in sanitation buckets or fresh poultry manure, spread it. Where there is ground to spare in a neglected garden, summer green manuring is a good way of improving the soil.

The best summer green manure, if you can spare the space, is the annual lupin (*Lupinus angustifolius*), which not only has efficient nitrogen-fixing bacteria in its roots, but also symbiotic fungi that reach out and make phosphates available. It contains an alkaloid which makes the large seeds distasteful to birds, and rabbits dislike the foliage, both garden advantages, but it is not such a good weed suppressor as the other green manures.

Sow the seeds singly in dibber holes 1 inch (2.5 cm) deep, 6 inches (15 cm) apart and 8 inches (20 cm) between rows, in the first week in April. Let them grow on, hoeing between the rows to kill off weed seedlings, and mow them in July, planting Brussels sprouts in the undug soil. Another trick is to sow sweetcorn between the lupin rows in May after hoeing, and to leave the corn to take advantage of the nitrogen and the *phosphorus* gathered by the lupins which will be suppressed by the stronger and later crop. An April sowing of lupins can also be dug under in August, in time for planting a new strawberry bed.

Annual blue lupin root, showing nitrogen fixing nodules

Organic pest control in September

September is not too soon to replace the cloth bands that trap the two-way traffic of caterpillars up and down your trees, with the grease bands against the winter moth (*Operophtera brunata*), the march moth (*Alsophila aescularia*) and the mottled umber moth (*Erannis defoliaris*). All three have wingless females and the first hatches between early October and December from pupae in the soil, climb apples, pears, plums and cherries to lay eggs high among the branches. These produce green, brown or yellow-green 'looper' caterpillars that hatch to eat leaves as soon as these have developed from the buds, enter the flower trusses and later attack leaves and developing fruit, dropping to the ground to pupate in June.

The mottled umbers start climbing in October and finish in February when the march moth begins and continues climbing until April when it has to feed fast to catch the June pupation season.

Any one of these three – or any combination of them – can build up a population capable of destroying an entire crop and permanently weakening the trees. The eggs resist winterwashes, and spraying the caterpillars needs strong pesticides just when the bees are on the blossom, and the *Anthocoris* at their most active.

So put on the grease bands in September and leave them on until the end of April, tying them tightly top and bottom about $3\frac{1}{4}$ feet (1 m) above ground level and taking care to see that no hollow in the trunk provides a safe subway underneath them. Check the bands at intervals to see that dead leaves or twigs have not blown against them, providing a bridge for the determined females to crawl across. This is an ideal organic answer, but must be done accurately.

CHAPTER 13
OCTOBER

October is the storing month, when the last of the roots for lifting come up with care to store in boxes because some, like carrots, keep better that way, and others for convenience, because digging slender scorzonera or tapered parsnips, like Tender and True, on a clay soil with fine snow blowing on the wind is not a task to linger over. If possible, leave roots in the ground, to save shed space, and be thankful that the cabbage tribe will take the worst our winters can fling at them, though American gardeners have to store even their broccoli in root cellars which are becoming increasingly rare in an age of home canning and deep freezing.

Peat is still the most popular storage medium, bought in bales, chopped down with a spade and watered, then shovelled to mix in the moisture, for it should not be too dusty dry or it will extract moisture from the vegetables. It is best to buy the peat well before lifting and leave it about three days after chopping to get it just moist enough to be thirsty. The problem of using fine ashes from solid-fuel central heating is that although these are mostly silica and alumina (unlike high-potash woodstove ashes) and cost nothing, they are inclined to get the roots too dry. Beetroot, carrots, swedes and turnips should all store in containers with the chosen medium spread in a layer on the bottom, and the roots set out in it with about ½-inch (1 cm) gap all round each. Then add more peat or ashes to allow a clear inch (2.5 cm) of the medium before the next layer of roots

goes in.

Real tea-chests are increasingly scarce and sell expensively for packing crockery and books on moving days. One way round the problem is to collect the white plastic, one-gallon (or 4 l) liquid containers (such as those holding shampoos and setting fluids used by ladies' hairdressers) and saw off the tops. These containers are oblong and about 1 foot (30 cm) high and though they are on the small side and use rather more peat proportionately, there is no risk of root rot spreading and no need to delve in deep peat to find the bottom layers. Select the contents which will probably be about as many as you would normally fetch and fill the container as suggested. Pack these together in a tea-chest size block, and put the next layer set across them, so they bond together like a brick wall without toppling over. As the containers are translucent white, cover them with old blankets to exclude light.

Potato storage

Potatoes breathe much more than other roots and therefore need no peat or ashes. Ideally they should go in jute sacks, but these can no longer be obtained and plastic always means condensation. The many-layered brown paper sacks in which even seeds are now sold are about good enough, especially covered with old blankets to exclude light. The essentials are to keep their temperature above the minimum 35°F (2°C) and to avoid the greenness from exposure to light that shows the pre-

Left *Convolvulus tricolor,* which furls its flowers at night, opens early in the morning providing hover-flies with dew and nectar breakfasts as they search your garden for aphid colonies and lay an egg in each.

Below left These discoloured gooseberry leaves do not show disease but potash shortage, common in sandy soils. Ground rock potash or comfrey is the answer, for many plant and human 'diseases' are dietary deficiencies.

Below Tomato leaves turning yellow, while the veins stay green, are less often virus-infected than they are lacking magnesium, because too much potassium fertilizer has locked this vital trace element out of reach of the tomato's roots.

Above Use a rotary mower to chop fallen apple leaves into 'bite-sized' portions for worms to take under with 85 per cent of the apple scab spores overwintering on them as worm equivalents of gourmet delicacies.

Left Our best and most versatile pest controller is *Anthocoris nemorum*. Barely an eighth inch (4 mm) long, it eats big bud and other mites and newly hatched caterpillars. Only use sprays that spare our smallest friend.

Below Robins follow digging gardeners, their beady eyes watching for the turned up tiny pupae of many pests. Your local pair will soon be tame enough to feed selectively by hand through hard winters.

Table 24: VEGETABLES FOR OCTOBER EATING

Available for eating	Family	Sowing	Planting
Beans, French	7	May	—
Beans, runner	7	—	May
Beetroot (fresh)	2	March	—
Cabbage	4	June	July
Carrots (early)	12	March	—
Carrots (maincrop)	12	April	—
Cauliflowers	4	February	April
Celery	12	March-April	May-June
Kale	4	April	June-July
Kohlrabi	4	March-April	—
Lamb's lettuce	13	May	—
Landcress	4	May	—
Leeks	8	April	July
Lettuce	3	May	—
Marrows; Courgettes	5	April	—
Miner's lettuce	10	May	—
Onions	8	March	—
Onions (spring)	8	August	—
Parsnips	12	February-March	—
Peas (maincrop)	7	April	—
Potatoes (maincrop)	11	—	April-May
Pumpkins	5	April	May
Radishes	4	March-August	—
Salsify	3	March	—
Scorzonera	3	March	—
Spinach, New Zealand	1	March	—
Spinach (summer)	2	April	—
Sweetcorn (fresh)	6	April-May	—
Tomatoes (outdoor)	11	—	May

sence of the alkaloid solanine. Frosted potatoes develop a most unpleasant, sweetish taste, which can be removed by putting them in a temperature of 60-65°F (15-18°C) for several days. Solanine can produce symptoms like gastric influenza if green potatoes are eaten in quantity, and in quite small amounts by those who are extra sensitive.

Seed potatoes are not harmed by exposure to light, which, in fact, improves them by increasing sprouting, but care should be taken to cover any exposed tubers when earthing up or when growing on the 'no-dig' system. It takes long exposure to light to turn potatoes green and this process can be reversed by storing them in complete darkness until they return to normal. In the USA, with a warmer and longer 'fall' than our often wet and cold autumns, they spread out newly harvested potatoes in layers one-spud thick in a sheltered place away from rain and wind at a temperature of 60-65°F (15-18°C) for a week and then turn them over to give the other sides a turn. This is called 'curing' and is intended to thicken their skins, heal any grazes or scratches from lifting and improve the keeping qualities of maincrops and second earlies for storing. Potatoes show the greatest difference between organically and chemically grown, so it is worth taking trouble to store them as carefully as apples. We could try the American curing method easily in an empty conservatory or sunny spare room.

Green tomato ripening

Green tomatoes also need care, for each is as alive as a fertile egg, and in our climate we can easily have four times as much of the crop left unripe as we have eaten red and ripe. Tomatoes contain fruit acids that tenderize meat as well as being a useful supply of vitamins and minerals for soups and stews right round the year, and are one of our most useful storing crops. Set out the green fruit in paper-lined chitting trays, on their sides and not touching each other, and cover them with oblongs of dressing-gown wadding, which is rather cheaper than cotton-wool and should last for years. Lift the trays off the stack once a week, remove the wadding (which will not catch on the stalks as these are sideways), pick out the ripe ones for cooking or bottling, and replace it.

This system will keep tomatoes ripening slowly into January, but with Harbinger, or any other fast ripener, most will come on fast enough on the plant to bottle or freeze before decay sets in. If frost merely threatens, pick all full-sized fruit from pale pink to cream in colour, and leave the smaller sizes unpicked for another week or ten days. Ripening on the plants makes all the difference to the taste, and real tinies never come to much in the end.

Apple storage

Apples need to have their stems left on, and the strictest attention paid to the period in season of every variety. Because no gardener can afford a cold store or a gas-tight room to pump full of carbon-dioxide, we have to ripen as they did in the past, handicapped by our lack of horses.

The ideal apple storage temperature is 32°F (0° C) with 80-90 per cent humidity, and at 40°F (5°C) they will only keep half as long. If the storage room is well insulated, and you have an old refrigerator that is still working (or can 'lend' yourself your own), put it in during the day time with its door open and cool the room down to give the newly picked apple harvest a good cold start. Shrivelling is caused by too low humidity or too high a temperature. It pays to have a length of old blanket hanging in a jam jar of water to keep up the humidity for all the storage areas. The old idea of wrapping each apple in newspaper worked by keeping the air next to the skin saturated with the moisture the apple itself breathed out. The problem is that unwrapping and rewrapping every apple in the trays is so slow that it is done too seldom to discard any that are rotting off and spreading spores. Going through the trays quickly once a week when you select for eating, means that it is done in time.

Starting a herb bed

Like orchards, herb beds are planned ahead, and October is a good month for dividing up the perennials, especially mint (*Mentha spicata*) and its many sub-species and varieties to be found in any herb catalogue. Collect plastic honey or ice-cream containers, and melt small holes in the bottoms, fill them with garden soil and sink them in the herb bed. This method enables you to grow a collection of assorted mints while keeping them from swarming through each other.

A herb bed is outside the rotation, and is ideally sited near the kitchen door, for nipping out and snipping just a sprig of something. It needs careful digging to remove all perennial weeds, but no special manuring, for all herbs produce the best flavours on poor soils. Nearly all of our herbs come from the dry, Mediterranean countries and they are easily overfed. Pot marjoram (*Origanum onites*) and thyme (*Thymus vulgaris* or the lemon-scented *T. citriodorus*) can both be divided in October, but the best way to obtain herbs is to raise them from seed, sown in April in labelled part-rows.

There is such a demand for herbs that the surplus seedlings can be sold off at fetes for worthy causes (after replanting when they are large enough to handle, 3 inches [8 cm] apart each way) or potted on in yogurt cartons for sale. Young plants from seed last and yield far better than divisions torn off large clumps. The following are all good standard herbs to use in soups, salads and general cookery. The natural orders of each are given, so that people with allergies can use them as flavours, though their common characteristic is strongly tasting alkaloids or essential oils and these cannot provide a real contribution to any diet.

Balm or **lemon balm** (*Melissa officinalis: Labiatae*) is fully hardy, but comes up more slowly than the others in this easy group.

Basil (*Ocimum minimum: Labiatae*) is a half-hardy annual described earlier.

Burnet (*Sanguisorba minor: Rosaceae*) is a perennial, used as a tea or to give a slightly cucumber flavour to salads.

Chervil (*Anthriscus cerefolium: Umbelliferae*) is an annual that runs to seed fast

like spinach, but should be sown thinly in rows 8 inches (20 cm) apart, thinned to 6 inches (15 cm) between plants, and snipped off just above the root six to eight weeks after the first sowing in March. This will provide another cut, but leave some of the first to run to seed – providing some for a July sowing and some for the following year. It is used in soups and salads, and freezes better than it dries.

Chives (*Allium schoenoprasum: Liliaceae*) is a small, perennial onion to snip for leaves to flavour almost anything. Increase by dividing the clumps in March or April. It can be raised from seed but rarely is because it is so prolific that it edges kitchen-garden beds.

Fennel (*Foeniculum vulgare: Umbelliferae*) grows very large and strong. Sow seed in pinches about 8 inches (20 cm) apart in a colony of four, and thin to the best. This is the tallest herb and should go at the back of the bed for leaves to use in sauces, soups and salads, and seeds to gather for a tea.

Rosemary (*Rosemarinus officinalis: Labiateae*) is an evergreen shrub that grows best in shelter on the south side of a house because it is not fully hardy. A sprig of rosemary can be added to the water when cooking peas or potatoes and placed inside roasting birds. It can be raised easily from seed sown like the others, but those who wish to take a 'Rosemary for Remembrance' from a friend, should break off a 6-9 inch (15-20 cm) length shoot *downwards* so it has a 'heel' of the parent branch, in June, July or August, and stand this in a jam jar full of water. In a few weeks it will grow small, white roots, and can be planted in a sunny place and watered to give it a start.

Sage (*Salvia officinalis: Labiatae*) is easily raised from seed sown in April, but slow to germinate and therefore worth marking with radishes like parsnips. Thin to 6 inches (15 cm) apart and expect to raise fresh every three years for it much easier from seed than cuttings. **Summer savory** (*Satureia hortensis: Labiatae*) is an annual with a taste rather like sage, excellent in stuffing and soups as well as for adding flavour to some of the rather dull bean dishes in vegetarian diets. Sow it like chervil and take two cuts a year from an April and a July sowing.

All herbs are at their best for drying when the flowers are just starting to open, so cut the foliage then and hang in bunches with a brown paper bag over each and head downwards, to dry slowly indoors. When they are crisp, put them through a mincing machine if you want them in fine fragments, stalks and all, or rub them through your fingers before storing in screw-topped jars.

Organic fruit care in October
October sees the return of the leaf-curling plum aphid (*Brachycaudus-helichrysi*) from its summer holidays on a number of herbaceous plants to its winter home on plums and damsons.

Just as our commonest aphid, the blackfly of broad beans, overwinters on Viburnums and Euonymus, the pests of our weeds and wildflowers are now winging their way back to our tree and bush fruits as they did when these (or rather their ancestors) were 'Foods for Free' for there were pests long before there were gardeners.

The damson-hop aphid (*Phorodon humuli*) is a pest of both crops, so heavily sprayed in both occupations that it has become resistant to almost everything. The cherry black fly (*Myzus cerasi*) is distasteful to all ladybirds except the two spot species, which has square, cream-coloured spots on a black background, looking like a tiny round chessboard. It goes to work when it is back from feeding on the lady's bedstraw.

From mid September to mid October, look over your bush fruit for aphids. Do not expect alarming quantities. There will be just a few finding sap enough on the young shoots to support them while they lay the eggs that will produce new swarms in the spring.

RASPBERRY PRUNING
Prune raspberry canes to three heights

Spray with soft soap, which can harm no *Anthocoris* hunting for early mite eggs or ladybirds taking a last few meals before hibernation.

Raspberry pruning

It is also raspberry-pruning time. Cut the temporary ties that have held the young shoots growing since the fruited canes were removed, and choose the best five or six on each plant. Tie these to the wires, shortening them so they finish at three different lengths, to avoid crowding the blossom which is often at the ends, and remove the smaller canes completely. Then dig between the rows, turning under the grass and comfrey mulch, removing any canes that are growing between the rows, and give your local robins their first chance at the raspberry-beetle chrysalids. Dig again in January if you have time.

Planting and pruning of cane fruit

October is as good a month as November for raspberry planting, either for a bed in a new garden, or renewing an old one, for raspberries and blackcurrants only last twelve to fifteen years, unlike the twenty to thirty years for red and white currants or gooseberries. Choose an equally sunny site in another part of the garden, and dig in compost or manure generously, plus 8 ounces a square yard (220 g per 0.83 m²) of bonemeal to start the bed away well. Space is more important than manure, for raspberries are shallow rooters and can take plant foods and humus they need from surface mulches between their canes, but suffer if they are crammed closer together than their minimum of 4 feet (1.3 m) between rows and 1 foot (30 cm) between canes. If the rows go closer they will block the light from each other and the bees need sunlight to work the blossoms. If possible, site your rows in a north to south direction, so the sunlight falls *along*

them, rather than only on the one unlucky unshaded row that faces south.

Because raspberries root shallowly, and gather their food from the manure spread between the rows, they need only 3-inch (8 cm) deep trenches, about spade width with 1 foot-deep (30 cm) holes each end to hold their support posts which should be about 6 feet (2 m) long, with two cross-pieces nailed across the bottom of each. Make these 1 foot (30 cm) long and 2 inches (5 cm) wide, and creosote them, and the posts, thoroughly. Nail one cross-piece at the bottom on the side away from the row, and one a foot higher up, *facing* the row. Drill the posts to take the wire. Five wires are enough, and they serve to hold up the canes, however tall and heavy they become. Blackberries, loganberries and boysenberries all lie on their wires more heavily than raspberries, and need the same type of support system. If plain posts without cross-pieces are used, the weight of the canes will simply draw them together, but as the cross-pieces push in both directions (see diagram) they will stay firm for the life of the bed.

Lloyd George is the last of the old raspberry varieties and it can be either an early July cropper, pruned as described, or left unpruned and cut down to ground level in March or April to fruit in September and October the following year. September, Hailsham and Lord Lambourne are also autumn fruiting, but never as popular as the ordinary summer kinds, because there is rarely enough sun to bring out their flavour.

The raspberries that have driven out the old kinds are the Malling varieties, bred by the late Norman Grubb of East Malling Research Station. The best of the mid-June fruiters is Malling Exploit with very large, well-flavoured berries. Malling Enterprise follows Lloyd George, and is another fine, large-

2 by 1 inch (5 by 2.5 cm) timber

8 inches (20 cm) apart

48 inches (1.20 m)

Soil level

18 inches (45 cm)

2 by 1 inch (5 by 2.5 cm) cross-piece 9 inches (23 cm) long to push soil this way

9 inches (23 cm) long cross-piece to push soil this way

SUPPORTING POSTS FOR RASPBERRY WIRES

flavoured kind, while Malling Landmark is the latest of all, beating Norfolk Giant on crop and flavour.

East Malling Research Station has now produced Autumn Bliss, which may well become an organic gardener's favourite. It is an autumn-fruiting variety, without the lower yields and poor taste of the familiar September and Hailsham, starting earlier in August with larger, tastier fruit spread over a two-month picking season, and resistance to the raspberry aphid carrying the virus. It is naturally erect, growing up to 5 feet (1.5 m) high so needs 5 feet (1.5 m) between rows and to be planted

18 inches (45 cm) apart in the rows, to prevent height shading the blossom and reducing the size of your crop.

When the canes are completely dormant cut them down to ground level and burn them with all their pests and diseases, including the leaf and bud mite (*Eriophytes gracilis*), which is hibernating under the bud scales of the canes we must leave on the ordinary varieties to bear next summer's crop, and the eggs of the green capsid (*Lycogocoris pabulinus*) are in there with them. This creature eats little brown specks on the leaves that become networks of holes.

Best of all, Autumn Bliss blossoms

too late for the raspberry beetle, which stops work in July to lay eggs in the flowers, which means no more grubs in them and no more worry about timing your sprays to miss the bees and catch the tiny caterpillars before they are safe inside the fruit. Dig in the grass and leafmould mulch between the rows that keeps the bed weed-free (your robins with their occupation gone will nonetheless find plenty of pupae to eat in the rest of your garden).

Raspberry canes are usually shaped like 'L's when they arrive, with the short arm the root. Place this along the 3-inch (8 cm) deep trench, fill in the soil, firm it well and tie the cane to the wires. This must not be allowed to fruit, but should be cut to 6-inch (15 cm) height in May before it blossoms because its function is to produce the leaves that feed the young canes which will be growing ready to tie in next August and prune the following October. Leaving the new canes to fruit will be such a strain on the plants that it will be two more years before the bed produces a crop worth picking.

Pruning trailing soft fruit
Before tying in the young canes on the loganberries and boysenberries, look round the bases of the thornless varieties (which are the best), and cut off any *thorned* shoots, for these can take the strength of the plant like suckers from the briar at the base of a rose. Do not shorten the main new shoots, for they will produce blossom bunches along their whole length, but tie them to cover the whole support structure. Leave room at the bottom of the structure for tying in the young shoots that will grow next summer ready to train up as replacements. If any of these trail very low, remove about six leaves 1 foot (30 cm) up from the growing point, and place a brick where the leaves were. The shoot should root into the

soil ready for removal to grow another plant for extending the soft-fruit beds.

The best flavoured blackberry is Himalayan Giant, but it is strong, very thorny and fruits as they all do on the old and young wood, but not all on the inside of the tangle that they struggle to become. The best time to prune them is December, because by then they will have dropped all their leaves and it is possible to see what you are doing and to do it with thick gardening gloves and stout secateurs. The best of the easy thornless kinds, which are small enough to fit on the same type of supports used for raspberries and loganberries, is Oregon Cutleaf Thornless, a sport off the old parsley-leafed variety.

The trailing berries need richer feeding than raspberries, and after clearing perennial weed roots from the 2-foot (60 cm) wide strip along which they should be planted, dig in 1 pound (450 g) of hoof and horn to every 6 feet (2 m) of this strip. Set the posts 6 feet (2 m) apart, and plant one loganberry, boysenberry or thornless blackberry in each. If you decide to have a Himalayan Giant, plant it by the central post and give it 6 feet (2 m) to spread along on each side. Shorten all the long shoots on the new plants to 15 inches (38 cm), or just enough length to tie them to the lowest wires. Cut these out when the new shoots from their bases are all well established and tie these in ready to fruit next year.

When the blackberries are bare, begin by cutting out any dead or really old branches that are crowing the younger shoots. Cut these out in sections, threading them out between the young shoots. When there is some room clear, train in the long, green, soft barked shoots that grew this summer, and tie them in. Some of the weaker of these will have to come out too, and in this case cut them through 2 inches (5 cm) below the surface, which gives a thornless 'handle' by which to pull out the thorny monsters. Bush-fruit prunings are among the items that should *never* be composted. Burn them, not only because of the thorns, but because they may contain pest eggs.

Autumn humus harvest

Autumn does not advertise so it is easy to forget the free humus harvest that is wasted on Council dumps and bonfires every year, and it is far less polluted than we think. Most of the lead from petrol falls within 100 feet (30.5 m) of the road, and there are hundreds of cemeteries, parks and sports grounds where piles of leaves are swept up each year at Council expense, well outside this distance. If you can get in touch with whoever is in charge of the leaf clearing exercise, you can usually get permission to collect them by the sackful. If your persuasive powers are really good and you can arrange for the street sweeping men to bring a lorry load, try to ensure that they are freshly collected.

Trees operate a 'giro system', throwing away the surplus minerals they draw through their roots through their leaves, from which other trees select the trace elements they require. This is how they can grow for centuries in the same place without running out of something scarce. No tree is looking for lead, cadmium, mercury or any of the metals with which industry pollutes the air, so that which falls on their leaves washes off and down in rain. Councils sweep leaves fairly soon after they fall, and October leaves are best.

These still have some carbohydrate and protein with their celluloses and hemicellulose, and if they are stacked as suggested earlier, either by one of the 'Hastening systems', or merely hosed and well packed, they will provide lasting humus for the future of your garden. You only absorb 15 per cent of the trace of lead your crops will take up from the fraction in your leafmould. If you live in a city you absorb 70 per cent of that in the air you breathe. However, Britain will not be able to continue to lead Europe in Air Pollution much longer and gardeners and others will rejoice.

CHAPTER 14
NOVEMBER

In November, the last sowings of the year are longpod broad beans for stored protein, not only to save time in the crowded spring, and give an earlier crop, but because there is some control of blackfly (*Aphis fabae*), due to the fact that the rather harder bark from the more mature growth makes only the tips attractive to the aphids, and these can be pinched out. This effect can be reinforced by sowing the beans on extra firm ground. Use a steel-shod dibber and plant without digging where autumn broccoli came out, or where the ground was trodden hard between outdoor tomato rows. With many of these time-honoured tricks we can only learn how good they are when we miss them for a season.

November is also the month for pruning and planting, digging in manure where trees and bush fruit will need it, rather than leaving land rough dug for the frost to break down, for research has show that more plant foods are wasted by washing out of bare ground on sandy soil that we gain by leaving clays rough dug for frost.

Planting and pruning blackcurrants
Blackcurrants are the best value for vitamin C from small gardens for the least trouble. Though Table 13 showed that Baldwin is highest, Westwick Choice comes a good second with 235 mg per 100 g, and also resists big bud mite, while Wellington XXX (third with 204) is a heavy cropper famous for flavour. Both have about a three-week picking season (spreading the bottling period),

with Westwick Choice later, and neither blossoms early enough to catch the worst frosts like the largest fruiting kind of all, Laxton's Giant, which is rare because so few people take the frost risk. Both are strong-growing kinds and are best planted 5 feet (1.5 m) apart each way to give plenty of room for picking. For very small gardens that can only spare 3 feet (1 m) apart, choose Amos Black, which is upright and small, fruiting late and well, but with rather more acid flavour than the first two.

Blackcurrants are nitrogen-greedy — therefore start them with manure rather than compost and as much as 2 pounds a square yard (1 kg per 0.83 m²) of hoof and horn if you have none. This is to give them a starting stock, for in small gardens it pays to diet your blackcurrants by keeping them to comfrey, mowings and leafmould on the surface in moderation, for chemicals, especially nitrogen, put their weight up so they grow out of our small gardens. Dig their holes 6 inches (15 cm) deep and wide enough to spread their roots flat in a disc, and firm the soil over these, ensuring that it comes up as far as the soil mark on the stem that shows how deep they were planted in the nursery.

Then cut back the shoots with light-brown bark that grew in the past summer to three or four buds — whichever points away from the centre. There will be no fruit next summer, which will be spent growing strong shoots from these buds, and these will fruit all the way up the following year.

They fruit best on this young wood,

Table 25: VEGETABLES FOR NOVEMBER EATING

Available for eating	Family	Sowing	Planting
Beans (dried or frozen)	7	May-June	—
Beetroot (fresh)	2	March	—
Cabbage	4	June	July
Carrots (early)	12	March	—
Carrots (maincrop)	12	April	—
Cauliflowers	4	February	April
Celery (self-blanching)	12	March-April	May-June
Kale	4	April	June-July
Kohlrabi	4	March-April	—
Lamb's lettuce	13	June-July	—
Landcress	4	July-August	—
Leeks	8	April	July
Miner's lettuce	10	June-July	—
Onions	8	March	—
Parsnips	12	February-March	—
Peas (dried or frozen)	7	January-May	—
Potatoes (maincrop)	11	—	April-May
Pumpkins (stored)	5	April	May
Radishes	4	March-August	—
Radish, Chinese	4	July	—
Salsify	3	March	—
Scorzonera	3	March	—
Spinach, New Zealand	1	March	—
Spinach (summer)	2	April	—
Sweetcorn (frozen)	6	April-May	—
Tomatoes (bottled)	11	—	May

which should be left full length, also on the two-year-old branches. In November remove about a third of the red-brown, barked branches that grew the previous summer and cut out any that are weak, or long and straggling, so they grow more long, straight shoots.

Pest and disease control by pruning
Many commercial blackcurrant growers use costly picking machines, cutting the bushes on half the field almost to ground level, sucking off the fruit for processing and chewing up the leaves and branches as a surface mulch. The cut down half spends the rest of the summer and the next season growing nothing but the long, light brown barked branches that fruit best, and the larger crop every other year gives almost the same yield as the two halves together on the old system, with a saving in labour for picking and pruning. Organic gardeners can modify the new method as a temporary pest and disease control measure that costs a year's crop from an afflicted bed.

Currant leaf spot (*Pseudopeziza ribes*) shows first as irregular brown blotches on the leaves in May and June that

BLACKCURRANT – WINTER PLANTING
Pruning a newly planted blackcurrant bush

increase faster in wet seasons until the leaves fall early, shrivelling the fruit and weakening the bushes. Small drops of liquid appear on the blotches which spread the disease through the summer. During the winter a second type of spore develops on the fallen leaves that is scattered in spring to blow on the wind and be splashed on low leaves by the rain. This disease is increasing, and so is that from gooseberry mildew, which is now attacking blackcurrants. Feeding the bushes extra nitrogen to make them grow heavier crops increases the risk, making a 'slimming diet' for your bushes the best protection.

If your bushes have the disease (it is quite unmistakable), pick the crop, which is entirely safe for eating unless you have tried to control the disease with something deadly within a month of picking, then use a pruning saw to cut back the bushes to 3 inch (7.5 cm) high stumps. The old organic answer was to collect the fallen leaves, but if these are burnt while they are still on the branches, this is far more effective. If there are any gooseberry mildew spores as well, put those on the bonfire too. Dig over between the bushes in the autumn to give the robins a really good chance at the gooseberry and blackcur-

rant sawfly pupae. If you cut down only half the bed, the infection carries over and you will have lost a year's crop for nothing. If you want to try the commercial system on a garden scale, use half a healthy bed of a single variety to give a fair comparison.

There are now two mildew-resistant types of blackcurrant both mid season varieties, yet blossoming late to dodge the frosts. Ben More blossom has stood 4°C (40°F) of frost without loss of its heavy crop of large fruit, held on stout and spreading branches, while Ben Sarek is an even heavier cropper but on smaller bushes. There are so compacted that the recommended spacing is 3 feet (1 m) apart each way in staggered rows.

There is no reason why organic gardeners who want their crop all at once for freezing should not use the trick that is making it a commercial favourite. When ripening is near, gather the branches together and tie them round with string. Cut the string when the outer fruits are really ripe and shake the branches. The fruit will all come pattering down onto spread polythene bags ready to tip into the basket. Try picking some in the normal way as they are ready and see if there is any difference, for the 'self picking blackcurrant' may be the fruit of the future – whatever the taste.

Red and white currants
Red and 'white' currants fruit on the old wood, like apples. Take back all the side shoots to three or four buds and shorten the leaders by about a third. This policy is all right for the first three prunings, but it means that the bushes grow bigger and bigger, so remove the longest and most straggling shoots each year, as though they were blackcurrants, to start more light-grey-barked young shoots low on the bushes.

Laxton's No. 1, which is early, and

Red Lake for later are both strong-growing kinds with a good flavour, while Versailles is the last of the white varieties still in cultivation. The best way to grow them is trained up a wall, so they can be protected by a nylon net, and grown in beds too narrow for anything else. Trained or cordon currant canes are very expensive today, but it is easy to grow your own.

Select the best of the young shoots that grew the previous summer on the pruned-off branches, cut them off with a 'heel' of older wood, and shorten them if they are longer than 1 foot (30 cm); 8 inches (20 cm) or 6 inches (15 cm) is about the best length. Make a cut with a spade along a garden line, insert the cuttings along it 2 inches (5 cm) apart and 4 inches (10 cm) deep, and tread the soil firmly back. They are rooted and growing by the following autumn, ready to cut back to six buds and transplant at 1 foot (30 cm) spacing. By the second autumn they will be ready for their permanent homes against the wall.

Shorten the new shoots only by about a quarter of their length, to the first strong bud that points along the wall, and take off any others that point away from it to the lowest along the wall-pointing one. The next year they will produce a few bunches of currants, and some side shoots. Pinch out their tips in July to put more strength into the fruiting buds round their bases, and when the leaves fall in November cut them back to about 1 inch (25 cm) length, shortening the leaders by 25 per cent. Wall redcurrants are uncommon, but they will live for many years, fruiting freely on the old wood providing they are pruned hard and trained flat, so the sun can ripen the wood for fruiting. It cannot ripen in the middle of an overgrown mass.

REDCURRANT FAN – WINTER PRUNING

Black, red and white currants all need the same manuring, but the last two should have even less nitrogen, for giving in to the greed of your currants makes them more liable to attack by *Septoria ribis*, the leaf-spot fungus which can make the leaves start falling in June and July in wet summers, with fruit withering. If this happens, spray with burgundy mixture in November. The fungus spores winter on fallen currant leaves, and as all three can only be forked over very shallowly because of their shallow roots, water the fallen leaves with urine on the apple-scab principle. This will not give too much nitrogen, because it will all be spent by the time the roots are feeding again.

Gooseberry planting and pruning

Gooseberries can also be trained up walls, either on a single stem or 'cordon' – which allows room for perhaps a dozen kinds for those who are starting a gooseberry collection, or fan trained. They are, however, so prickly that the hard pruning they need becomes a burden. They fruit on the old wood like redcurrants, and need the same soil treatment, but with the addition of 1 pound a square yard (450 g per 0.83 m^2) of rock potash on sandy soils. This newly available mineral is the answer to the problem of growing gooseberries in Rhododendron and heather-type gardens in Surrey, but on clays they do well with comfrey if they run low. The symptoms of potash hunger in gooseberries are leaves turning a blue-green, with light-brown edges that look as though they have been scorched.

The main gooseberry problem is weeding under the bushes and Careless, the commonest kind, seems to be so named because it does not care how badly it scratches its owner. Choose Whitesmith instead, which is upright, resists American gooseberry mildew, and fruits rather earlier, ripening to

amber yellow, or Langley Gage, equally resistant and upright, green ripening to cream with the finest flavour of all. For a red kind, with flavour, upright habit and mildew reistance, buy Bedford Red, which is the tastiest, but has a smaller crop. These three are the best of the two-hundred-odd known gooseberries rapidly being driven out of cultivation by Careless, which is large fruited, heavy cropping and so savage that some day gooseberry pickers' strikes may drive it off the market.

Plant the bushes 4 feet (1.3 m) apart each way, 6 inches (15 cm) deep and the roots spread like those of blackcurrants, with the soil well firmed. Order your bushes early, and offer to pay extra for specimens with extra long 'legs'. A gooseberry's leg is the length of brown trunk from where the roots spread to the first branches, and the longer it is the more room there will be to reach under for weeding. After planting, cut back the light-brown barked shoots to between three and five buds, which gives scope to choose one that points up and away from the centre as the end one, which will grow a new shoot rather than blossom.

In the November after planting, shorten these new shoots to about 8 inches (20 cm) long and take out completely any that are growing towards the middle. The best shape for a gooseberry bush is that of an empty ice-ceam cone, and this is easy enough if you buy an upright variety and train it so the sun can get into the middle to ripen the wood and the fruit and you can reach in to pick it without bloodshed.

There is now a highly mildew-resistant gooseberry bred by East Malling Research Station. It is called Invicta and produces large fruit that ripen yellow for raw eating, rather like Careless but with twice the crop over the same season. It is excellent for cooking, jam

GOOSEBERRY PRUNING

making, freezing and raw eating ripe, but with one large snag. It is too strong and prickly for the pick-your-own trade, perhaps the thorniest gooseberry ever bred. It is best grown as double or single cordons 1 foot (30 cm) apart against a wall where it can be kept flat by summer pruning, so the fruit can be picked as easily as tomatoes.

Gooseberries do well on north walls, fruiting rather later than those facing south, which gives two ripe picking seasons for a collection of dessert varieties, on a bed that need only be 8 inches or 1 foot (20 or 30 cm) wide. Choose Bedford Red, Crown Bob (also mildew resisting), large, dark red, Howards Lancer – a large, yellow fruit of good flavour – Langley Gage, the sweetest of the yellows, Leveller – a yellow known as the 'Cox's Orange Pippin' of

gooseberries when the Cox was new and gooseberries were cherished not only for size but flavour – and Whitesmith – with a superb taste ripening as white as white wine.

Feed them as though they were tomatoes, starting the bed with 1 pound per square yard (0.45 kg per 0.83 m^2), or 9 feet (2.74 m) of bed of rock potash, spreading about 1 ounce per foot (28 g per 30 cm) of woodash under a mulch of lawn mowings each spring, and water with comfrey liquid manure when the crop is swelling to ripeness.

Cherries on walls
The best place for cherries in modern gardens is trained on walls away from the vandalism of modern birds, and a nylon net curtain is cheaper than a

fruit cage for cherries hung with snow. The cherry problem is that most sweet, eating varieties need pollen partners, and few houses have enough window-free wall for more than one.

Morello, the easy, hardy, cooking kind, can train on a north or even an east wall, and is completely self-fertile. Though the Duke cherries sometimes fruit alone, this is chancy and they are not very sweet. The new Canadian variety, Stella, the first self-fertile sweet cherry and which has strong and solid branches, is the answer. Buy one as a 'maiden', which is a year-old tree, and cut the main leader out after planting in November, with care to protect the cut with Bineb powder to defeat dieback or other spores. Then train the small side branches along the wall, tying them back to the vine eyes (like big screweyes) in rawlplugs that should hold the faulty telephone wire which is best for training all fruit, for the insulation is softer than the thin plastic on 'garden wire', which rubs through bark and causes canker.

During the summer tie any side shoots to the wires and pinch back any that point out, or any that race up fast from low on the tree, to buds that point along the wall. Cherries fruit most on one- and two-year old wood, so do not need spur-pruning like apples. Cut out broken or sickly branches, or those that have ceased to fruit; otherwise stick to dieback removal, and pinching or snipping soft shoots in summer and tying in. If you have room for two cherries, plant Bigarreau Napoleon and Frogmore Early, both red and yellow and fruiting in June and July. They have large blossom which makes a fine show against a red brick wall.

Plum programme

Plums are also good wall fruit and, like cherries, will fruit on north or east walls, leaving the south and west for peaches, apricots or nectarines. Oullin's Golden Gage is self-fertile, and so is Czar, but only a cooker or bottler. If there is room on an east wall, plant Coe's Golden Drop and Count d'Althan's Gage, both delicious golden plums to eat in September. Kirke's Blue, reputedly the finest-flavour plum, needs a south wall, or a southern garden, and Cambridge Gage, perhaps the best-flavoured greengage of all, as a pollen partner.

Two feet (60 cm) is about the minimum width for stone-fruit border, for this allows space to dig out a trench to hold lasting plant foods. Make this 3 feet (1 m) long, 2 feet (60 cm) deep and 18 inches (45 cm) wide, bringing it out clear of any concrete foundations. Fortunately, stone fruit have relatively weak roots compared with poplars and do not creep under the house into subsoil. A good supply of slowly available food keeps the roots at home if they have any tendency to wander.

Take out any builder's rubbish you find and wheel it away with the subsoil, which is the main reason for digging so deep. Then mix 4 pounds (2 kg) of bonemeal and 6 pounds (3 kg) of oystershell chicken grit (except on chalk soils) and scatter about half this on the bottom of the hole, tread in firmly 6 inches (15 cm) of good garden soil, add the rest of the mixture and then fill in with more good garden soil. If the soil is very bad, buy a few lawn turves (which will have good loam under them and be quite cheap if fetched from a garden centre) and pack them, grass down, in the bottom of the hole.

Keep the trunk of the trained tree away from the wall, so it is possible to get a syringe behind it, and above all do not forget to keep the bed level well below the damp course. Grease-banding is not easy on trained trees, because ants and many other creatures simply walk up the wall. The answer is to paint a strip of grease-band material along the wall, not right round the house but below the trees.

It is expensive to use a modern tree-grease on this scale, so the following old-fashioned recipe for a do-it-yourself grease is suggested. Mix together 8 parts of powdered resin, 4 parts linseed oil, 4 parts turpentine and ½ a part of honey; bring the mixture slowly to boiling point, and paint it on the wall while still hot.

The easiest stone fruit for any wall is the red cherry-plum, and its yellow variety. Both are self-fertile, with fruit about the size of nutmegs and the disadvantage of cropping very well one year and missing the next. These plums were once grown for the tall hedges that sheltered Somerset cider orchards, planted 3 feet (1 m) apart, with stakes between each and woven into a kind of basket work by the hedgers. If cherry-plums can be found (there are firms that stock them still), prune merely by removing dieback, and tie the shoots into the wires to ripen their wood and its fruit behind a nylon net. It is the only stone fruit that can be cut back carelessly, and it has even been pruned by farmworkers with long hedging bills as issued to the Somerset Home Guard in 1940 as well as Monmouth's men. It bottles well, makes jam and is sweet when ripe; larger than a cherry, much smaller than a greengage, and unfamiliar to modern greengrocers and housewives.

Damsons also make a hedge, but again the problem is that the birds strip the buds before you have hardly even seen the blossom. Farleigh is the hedge damson, to plant 3 feet (1 m) apart and crowd itself tall like a Leyland Cypress (*Cupressus leylandii*), the fastest evergreen hedge which only gives gardeners satisfaction till its fifteenth year, when it is too big for anything but firewood. Treat Farleigh as a hedge, clipping back the bare branches in November, and chancing the loss of the crop. Merryweather is also self-fertile and can be trained on a wall (with a fruit net to protect it) by those who like damsons, which are on the sharp side but excellent for wine and damson cheese.

All stone fruits need lime, because the bulk of their stones is calcium, and the rest is largely potash, but their deep roots keep up the supply. They can become short of nitrogen, yielding small fruit, with larger stones than normal, which is a sign that they need deep-litter poultry compost or any other manure, spread beneath – but not touching – the trees. Those who can plant standard plums should choose bush specimens of self-fertile Victoria, or Kirke's Blue, with Belle de Louvaine, its other good pollinator. Make the holes 2 feet (60 cm) square and deep; drive the stout stakes 1 foot (30 cm) deep in the bottom of the holes, and fit the roots round them, for if stakes are driven in after planting they may damage the roots.

CHAPTER 15
DECEMBER

The year ends with time to plan ahead and look through the diary that every gardener should keep, to see what went wrong and what went right, of what we grew too little and what we sowed too late. Some of us may decide to give up maincrop potatoes because they are easily bought. Others feel that freshness, flavour and freedom from pesticides are all-important and that it is better to grow the maximum quantities of the bulky vegetables that include potatoes as well as salads right round the year, even if we have to slaughter the shrubs and abolish the lawn. We dug it up for Victory once – we could dig it up now for healthier food.

It is likely that as allergies increase with rising pollution from pesticides, fumes and increasing numbers of additives, many more of the unfortunate people who are sensitive to even traces of these substances will form co-operatives through which those of them who have no gardens can be sure of getting what their health demands. In Switzerland these are already working successfully, with members paying a fixed annual sum for vegetables round the year; this covers the costs of including gardeners' wages, and works out at about wholefood shop prices – far less than for any individual employing a gardener to grow the family supply.

The HDRA publishes a directory of organic farmers, market gardeners and other organically grown produce suppliers, but bought foods cannot be as cheap as growing as much of your own food as possible. The major problem is one of running an alternative food distribution system to the mammoth chain of markets, processors and wholesalers that carry the products of factory farms and agribusiness enterprises to the supermarkets. This is not insoluble, however, because not only is small beautiful, it can be vastly cheaper in many ways. Organic growers in many areas are organizing 'consumers' clubs' where produce can be brought to a central depot and collected, for few smallholders can spare the time to stand at market-stalls waiting for customers.

Today we live at the end of food chains that reach right round the world. We expect to be able to eat oranges, lemons, bananas and apples every day of our lives without thought of season or distance. There is no way in which we can build up an alternative apple-chain fast enough from New Zealand, South Africa, Tasmania and Canada to replace sprayed fruit with unsprayed. We shall have to return to enjoying our own apples and pears in their seasons, as each kind comes to perfection, taking also what the organic growers of the world can offer us.

Of course this depends on whether we can pay for it, for the cost gap between 'battery fruit' – pruned by spraying, fed by chemicals and harvested, graded and packed by machine – and the 'hand-grown' product from an organic orchard, will grow ever wider. More and more it is going to pay us to grow our own fruit.

We have here another variation of the potato problem. If we have small gar-

Table 26: VEGETABLES FOR DECEMBER EATING

Available for eating	Family	Sowing	Planting
Artichokes, Jerusalem	3	—	February-March
Beans (dried or frozen)	7	May-June	—
Beetroot (stored)	2	May	—
Beetroot (leaf)	2	April	—
Broccoli (heading)	4	May	July
Brussels sprouts	4	May	June-July
Cabbage	4	June	July
Carrots (stored)	12	May	—
Celeriac	12	March	May
Celery	12	March-April	May-June
Hamburg parsley	12	March-April	—
Kale	4	April	June-July
Lamb's lettuce	13	July-August	—
Landcress	4	August-September	—
Leeks	8	April	July
Lettuce	3	March-July	—
Miner's lettuce	10	July-August	—
Onions (stored)	8	March	—
Parsnips	12	February-March	—
Peas (dried or frozen)	7	January-May	—
Potatoes (stored)	11	—	April-May
Pumpkins	5	April	May
Radish, Chinese	4	July	—
Salsify	3	March-April	—
Scorzonera	3	March-April	—
Spinach (winter)	2	September	—
Swedes (stored)	4	July	—
Sweetcorn (frozen)	6	April-May	—
Tomatoes (bottled)	11	—	May-June
Turnips (stored)	4	June-July	—

dens, should we give up the major part of our room to growing enough apples to keep 0.3 per cent of a doctor away every day, or should we concentrate on fresh salads, carrots (which are the most heavily sprayed of all the vegetable factory products) or potatoes with which you really tell the difference by the flavour?

The answer is a matter of taste, space and personal choice in the only area in our lives in which all our choices can be purely personal. We can, if we wish, plant the banners of an ever-growing army of apples that are important because they are our own. Let us sound the first blast of the trumpet against the monstrous regiment of Golden Delicious, and its polythene-skinned, sugared-water-blooded, paint-bright partners. The important fact about Cox is not that it has a short name everyone knows and it sells well if it is packed, graded and marketed well; it is that

Mr Richard Cox (1776-1845) of Lawn Cottage, Colnbrook, Slough, a retired brewer, grew it from a pip he sowed *in his own garden*. The tree itself blew down in 1911, but its grafting wood goes marching on in the orchards and gardens of the world. Great apples are like great music – they happen rather seldom, but their performance can be ruined by a poor conductor and an under-rehearsed orchestra.

Planting apples and pears

The place for fruit trees is at the bottom of the garden, partly because you will be fetching vegetables every day from the kitchen garden, and your fruit less often, but also because you can see the blossom better from the bedroom windows. Standard apples, pears and plums (if you risk the birds) need to go 16 feet (5 m) apart each way, and 10 feet (3 m) from each row end, which allows a maximum of two rows of four in the bottom 74 feet (22 m) of the average semi-detached house garden. Bush trees are cheaper and on a dwarfing stock such as Malling IX, or M.M. 106 (which not only keeps trees small but gives resistance to woolly aphid), they can go 10 feet (3 m) apart each way and 6 feet (2 m) at row ends. This allows three rows of six in 72 feet (21 m), if you cut out the central path down the middle of the garden.

If you order your standards early while there is still a choice, ask for 'extra tall', for nothing is worse when you are near 6 feet (2 m) tall, than to have to duck each time you mow under the trees. Choose standards with 6-7 feet (about 2 m) from the soil mark on the trunk that shows how deep they were planted in the nursery, to the spread of the first branches. Each tree, bush or standard needs 1 square yard (0.83 m²)

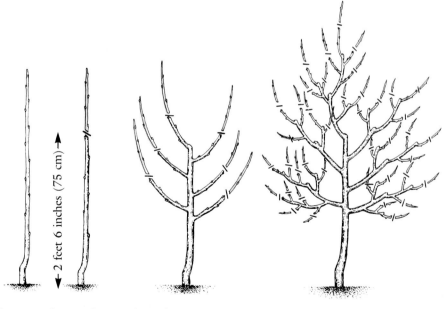

First year: shorten the 'maiden' or single shoot tree

← 2 feet 6 inches (75 cm) →

Second year: cut back side shoots to 3-5 buds

Third year

DWARF PYRAMID PEAR/APPLE PRUNING

of bed round it which can be planted with daffodils, but not much else can grow there. Half-standard trees need the same spacing, and are excellent for running chickens under as they keep the crop out of pecking range.

Dwarf pyramid apples produce the greatest weight of crop off the smallest space, and as they start as 'maidens' or one-year-old grafted trees, these are cheaper and do not require the structure of support posts demanded by cordons – the other system of packing maximum fruit into minimum space. They are planted 4 feet (1.2 m) apart and 9 feet (3 m) between rows, which should run north and south so the sunlight falls along them. The space between the trees is left bare, a 6-foot (2 m) strip is grassed down and mown between rows, and the apples grow as a kind of fruiting hedge about 7 feet (2 m) high. They are grown on dwarfing stocks and summer pruned as described for July.

Dig the holes well in advance 2 feet (60 cm) square and 18 inches (45 cm) deep, for up the bottom and drive home the stakes before planting as recommended earlier. Bush trees need short, stout stakes to come up as far as the fork of the branches, and dwarf pyramids need one that reaches about 4 feet (1.2 m) above ground level. Remove the subsoil from the bottom of the planting hole and replace with better soil, even if you have to buy turf, because nothing repays a good start more than apples and pears.

These trees are not in such need of lime as stone fruit, but they do need magnesium so, instead of chicken grit, spread 2 pounds (1 kg) of dolomite in each hole, with bonemeal and hoof and horn. On sandy soils add 2 pounds (1 kg) a hole of rock potash, for trees stay a long time in one place and appreciate a slowly released hoard of lasting minerals.

Standard and bush trees can be bought ready pruned, and if you ask when ordering in August or September, the nursery will have time to make a note to have this done. If not, cut back the smooth-barked wood that grew the

Cordons pack the most fruit into least space. They need stout posts and wires with 7 foot (2.15 m) bamboo canes to train along

previous summer by a third, finishing on a bud that points outwards, and shorten half the lesser branches or laterals to 2-3 inches (5-8 cm). Dwarf pyramids should be pruned as in the diagram. Make sure when shortening the leaders in winter that the central main leader is well above the others.

It takes two people to plant a tree, one to hold it and fit the roots spread on the bottom of the hole round the stake, and the other to fill back the soil carefully, working it among the roots and waiting to tread it until there is enough soil over the roots for your shoes not to damage the bark. Cut off the ends of any broken roots cleanly and be sure that the bulge which shows where the tree was grafted is well above ground level. It can root direct into the soil and 'undwarf' itself.

A choice of apples

Apples are the nicest source of easily storable vitamin C that can be grown in every garden, and offer all the minerals that are found in cider vinegar, which itself is a 'locker-up' of this important vitamin. They vary in how much they hold, as well as in taste, storing qualities, blossoming period and many other qualities. Table 27 is based on *Nutritional Values in Crops and Plants* by Professor Werner Schuphan (Faber and Faber, 1965). The months after each variety refer to those during which it will be ready for eating if stored at 1.5°C (35°F) and the correct humidity.

Northern Spy is sometimes imported from the USA and is a bargain in bought vitamin C, compared with Rome Beauty which is frequently in the shops. Golden Delicious is only 2.5 mg behind our Cox, but the difference in taste is as that between Coca Cola and good wine. It also needs a warmer climate than ours for full production, so even those who like it cannot grow it well themselves. The highest vitamin C

cooker is Golden Noble, but when cooked, an apple's vitamin C content is halved, so it comes down to a level between Cox and Lane's Prince Albert, but this is still far ahead of Bramley's Seedling, which comes down to just below Golden Delicious.

If you have room for only one apple choose Allington Pippin (October-December), which is one of the few self-fertile varieties, a good cooker as well as an acid and aromatic eater with a taste of Cox (one of its parents), and with a place above the bottom of the vitamin C league table. It is hardy, vigorous and a heavy cropper, with the added advantage that it will pollinate Cox well, for it blossoms at the same time, and if you decide you have room for another, you can have a Cox to go with it. Its eating season begins rather earlier, as shown by the months after its name and because it is a vigorous tree it should be grafted on M.M. 106. If there is room at the bottom of your garden to plant it 15 feet (5 m) from the end fence, have a standard rather than a dwarf pyramind, on Malling II.

Those who live in the far north, with a short growing season and late frosts, should choose Crawley Beauty (December-February) which also fruits alone, and is a fine frothy cooker, but will ripen to golden-yellow sweetness. It is the latest apple to blossom and thrives on cold clays. With room for two, plant also Court Pendu Plat (December-May) which produces small, yellow-fleshed fruit in quantity on a modestly growing tree, usually handicapped for lack of a pollen partner with the same late, frost-defeating blossom. It is an excellent apple for tough conditions, with about the same vitamin C content as Allington.

For less extreme conditions, north of a line from Birmingham to the Wash, where Cox fails to thrive, choose Laxton's Royalty (November-March)

Table 27: AVERAGE VITAMIN C CONTENT IN APPLES

Type (E = Eater, C= Cooker)	In Season	Vitamin C Mg per 100 g
Ribston Pippin (E)	Nov-Jan	30.60
Sturmer Pippin (E)	March-May	29.00
Golden Noble (C)	Sept-Jan	25.10
Orleans Reinette (E)	Dec-Feb	22.40
King of the Pippins (E)	Oct-Dec	18.10
Reinette du Canada (C or E)	Nov-April	17.20
Northern Spy (E)	Feb-May	16.70
Adam's Pearmain (E)	Dec-Feb	16.30
Bramley Seedling (C or E)	Nov-Mar	16.00
White Transparent (C or E)	August	15.30
Beauty of Bath (E)	July-Aug	14.00
Peasgood's Nonsuch (C or E)	Nov-Dec	13.20
Blenheim Orange (C or E)	Nov-Jan	13.20
Lane's Prince Albert (C)	Nov-Mar	12.70
Cox's Orange Pippin (E)	Nov-Jan	10.50
Gascoyne's Scarlet (C or E)	Sept-Jan	8.90
Worcester Pearmain (E)	Aug-Sept	8.20
Golden Delicious (E)	Nov-Feb	8.20
Bismark (C)	Nov-Feb	7.90
Court Pendu Plat (E)	Dec-May	7.50
Allington Pippin (E)	Oct-Dec	7.30
James Grieve (E)	Sept-Oct	6.80
Edward VII (C)	Dec-April	6.30
Laxton's Superb (E)	Nov-Feb	5.10
Early Victoria (C)	July-Aug	4.80
Rome Beauty (E)	May-June	3.80

which is a cross between Cox and Court Pendu Plat, with the late blossoming of the second parent and almost the flavour of the first. With it plant Winston (January-March), a good flavour eater, a strong grower and resistant to scab, as well as a late-blossoming frost dodger. With room for a third, make this Gascoyne's Scarlet (September-January), a vigorous tree, with soft, red-tinted flesh, and a good eater with a flavour, next to Cox on vitamin C. It is perhaps the best apple for a chalky soil, where Winston is also excellent. The two make an ideal couple for chalky gardens where they should ideally be grafted on Malling II, because Malling IX does not give them sufficient root-hold against winds that blow over big beaches. To make a fourth, add King of the Pippins (October-December), with a slightly bitter-sweet taste, a heavy crop, scab resistance and excellent vitamin C, and a good companion for Laxton's Royalty. Apple planting is not like collecting stamps – choose any two out of a group and add 25 per cent of any other as commercial growers do if you have the room.

The high vitamin C group all flower rather earlier than Cox or James Grieve, our two most popular apples. They are apples for the south and this is why they are not in every garden. The highest of all is Ribston Pippin (November-January) with a superb flavour, crisp, juicy and aromatic, but reputed to do best with *two* pollinators. Plant it with Adams' (not Worcester) Pearmain (December-March) with a 'Coxy' flavour and more vitamin C, and Egremont Russet (October-December) which has a good flavour, upright habit, and the russet-brown skin of this type of apple. For an early eater in place of any other group, choose Merton Charm (September-October), which is better flavoured than James Grieve and keeps better, but is new and scarce. Use the HDRA Fruit Finder Service for this or anything uncommon and not to be found in garden centres.

Sturmer Pippin is only 1.60 mg behind the winner and blossoms just right to pollinate Cox. It is a good cropper, a nice eater and a compact grower, which should be left to ripen on the tree as long as possible. Cox's Orange Pippin (December-May) is the finest-flavoured apple of all, but needs a well-drained soil (not a cold, wet clay) and a watch kept to see it does not run out of magnesium – the key sign is whether the leaves drop early but stay on at the tips of the young shoots. Spray with Epsom salts as suggested earlier or use dolomite at planting time or as a surface dressing. Rock potash is also appreciated, but chemical nitrogen leads to scab and canker.

As a pollinator for Cox, or for Sturmer Pippin (if you decide to be original and *not* plant Cox), James Grieve (September-October) is an early eater, but not a good keeper. Another with a flavour similar to Cox but much more resistant to cold is Kidd's Orange Red (November-February) which resists scab and mildew.

Among the leaders on vitamin C is Orleans Reinette (December-February),

a famous apple for flavour, good in the north and partly self-fertile, but it crops better with another late-blossoming kind. It is liable to scab and canker, but is mainly unpopular because its blossom period does not fit Cox. Plant it with Golden Noble, which will ripen for eating although on the sharp side, or Duke of Devonshire (January-March), which is firm, yellow and sweet, a good compact grower for small gardens and highly scab resisting. The HDRA publishes 'The Good Fruit Guide' (£2.25) which describes about 1,000 varieties of bush and tree fruit, with their pollinators, qualities and their suppliers.

A choice of pears

Pears are delicious, but need to be eaten when they are still juicy and mellow, before they go 'sleepy' or overripe. We are spoiled by being able to buy pears from cool storage almost all the year round, and have lost the art of judging the colour shade and softness that meant each variety was exactly right to eat with silver fruit knives. They are lower in vitamin C than apples, ranging from 4-7 mg like plums, and they blos-

Plant cordons on the slant with key to keep the graft above ground so they cannot 'undwarf' by rooting from above the dwarfing stock som earlier, so are more likely to catch frosts. As far as we know, no one has ever been allergic to pears so those concerned with allergy should plant pear trees.

We are rapidly becoming a one-pear country, for the excellent in horticulture is always the enemy of choice, and Conference, the long, tapered pear that everyone knows, has got everything for the amateur gardener, and nearly everything for the commercial grower. It is self-fertile, a strong grower, a heavy cropper, sweet and juicy and is at its best in October and November. Though Conference will crop with its own pollen, the fruit can be long and curly. If you are planting an organic orchard to provide fruit for sale, plant Josephine de Malines – very sweet with a delicious flavour, keeping until January, providing succession as well as shapeliness in its pollen partner.

The only other pear we have that is holding its own is Doyenné du Comice (November) with a better flavour but susceptible to scab. It needs a pollinator and since Laxton's Superb got firelight and had to be destroyed to prevent this bacterial disease which came from America killing all the pears in Britain, the best is Buerre Hardy (October). This is a vigorous, heavy cropper with a fine flavour, and autumn leaves that are a splendid red.

Dr Jules Guyot (September) is also self-fertile with a better flavour than Conference and as heavy a cropper, but resisting scab. Another self-fertile pear is Margaret Marillat (September), also a heavy cropper, rather like Conference in appearance but not such a good flavour, though sweet and juicy.

Choose your apples and pears with care, for you are buying thirty to fifty years of fruit and blossom; the price you pay for your trees will be doubled, if you accept a substitute from the nursery's stock which catches the frost in your garden and you then have to buy another. Unlike potatoes, which you can try new each year till you find the one that suits your taste and conditions, fruit trees are like good marriages – they can, with careful cultivation, grow in splendour of blossom, richness and delight in your garden, as long as you both shall live.

APPENDIX
THE HENRY DOUBLEDAY RESEARCH ASSOCIATION

The Henry Doubleday Research Association began in 1955 out of a book, a bear and a ton of lucerne seed. The book was my *Russian Comfrey* (now long out of print), which began modern comfrey growing in all countries, and the HDRA grew out of the fan mail it drew from farmers and gardeners all round the world.

In 1954 I sent the first modern comfrey from Mrs Greer's field to Canada, and Mr A. H. A. Lasker, the Canadian seedsman who bought it, sent me a ton of lucerne seed as a gift for my part in the epic struggle that got it across.

The lucerne was a variety barred to Britain by a dollar shortage and about the most awkward possible present for a struggling gardening writer, for it hit Regulation 365, which then controlled food parcels and laid down that gifts must weigh no more than 22 pounds (10 kg) and be 'for personal use only.' Such use would have required 50 acres (20 hectares) on which to sow the seed, and stock to eat it; but the £275 that a famous farm seedsman was willing to pay for it would be enough to start a research station.

Two MPs fought hard to get it through. There was a letter in the *New Statesman*, and an article in *Time and Tide* – but all in vain. Canada's gift lay at the London docks awaiting a British 'Boston Tea Party' – until a second generous gift arrived at the Regulation 365 barrier.

While the battle of the seed was raging, an American wild-animal dealer gave a nice, tame, black bear to an old friend in London, whose wife objected to its 'personal use' as a pet. Two hundredweight (100 kg) of bear, breaking the weight restriction, sitting up to beg dockers' sandwiches and posing with Teddy-bear appeal for Fleet Street photographers, soon crashed through the red-tape barrier. So it ambled to the children's corner of a zoo, closely pursued through the dock gates by a ton of lucerne seed.

With the money from selling the seed, I leased the Trial Ground at £10 a year when it was only ¾ of an acre (0.3 hectares), paid for the fencing, the labour cost of planting the comfrey presented by the comfrey growers of Britain, and the publication of *Comfrey Report No. 1* (now out of print). From that small beginning we have grown, until in 1958 we became a Registered Charity of the type that gives away knowledge rather than money.

In 1961 we appealed to our members (then only 470) and raised £1,500 towards the £2,500 needed to buy the freehold at building-landprice. Then a member of our committee, the late Dr Sidney Osborn of Ipswich, lent us £1,000, interest-free, to acquire the land for ever, with a long triangle reaching down towards a bird sanctuary and giving us just two acres (0.8 hectares). To our great regret, Dr Osborne died that winter, before we had begun paying back his loan, and left us the balance in his will. So, in part, our Bocking Trial Ground is a memorial to the doctor who brought the infant

HDRA into the world, and to the generosity of our members in many countries.

I christened the Association after Henry Doubleday (1813-1902) who was a Quaker, like his forbears who sailed with William Penn to Pennsylvania. One of his descendants founded Doubleday's, the American publisher, and his cousin Henry Doubleday of Epping made the first collection of butterflies for the British Museum. Henry Doubleday of Coggeshall introduced the hybrid he called 'Russian comfrey' from Russia in the 1870s, in the hope that its protein (called 'mucilaginous matter' in some of the early analyses) would replace the erratic supplies of gum arabic that were endangering his contract with the firm of De la Rue to supply gum for the later penny-black stamps and some of the early colonial issues.

Unfortunately, gummy proteins do not stick stamps; Henry lost his contract, and his small gum factory failed. He appears to have introduced an F_1 hybrid of comfrey which produced up to 100 tons an acre in Britain, and to have spent the last thirty years of his life experimenting with it. It was his dream that the crop would not only feed horses, cattle, sheep, pigs and poultry, but also solve the problem of world hunger, when that vision came not from biologist Paul Ehrlich but from the Irish Potato Famine of the 1840s. After his death, his relations cleared up after 'poor Uncle Henry', the dedicated elderly bachelor, and burned the records of his work. As I was determined that my work on comfrey, which began in 1948, should not be tidied away and lost, I founded the Association and named it in his honour.

The work of the Association soon grew far beyond the agricultural, horticultural, medicinal and nutritional uses of comfrey, and it has gone on growing until today it is the largest body in what is loosely called 'The Organic Movement' in Britain and probably the largest in the world. Its official objects are:

1. The improvement and encouragement of agriculture and horticulture generally.

2. Research into, and the study of, improved methods of organic farming and gardening.

3. Research into the utilization of Russian comfrey in connection with the foregoing objects.

4. The enouragement of research and experiment in agriculture and horticulture by, and the dissemination of knowledge of the results of such research and experiment among, farmers, gardeners and schools.

5. The advancement of knowledge of, and the fostering of public interest in, the benefits to be derived from the utilization of Russian Comfrey and other plants useful in organic husbandry.

It is a Research Association because a proportion of its members carry out experiments in their own gardens, as a hobby. These experiments are designed to find cheap, simple and effective answers to the problems of gardening using the fewest chemicals. Because this kind of research rarely has any prospect of finding anything to patent or sell, and is rarely carried out even by universities, it is still possible for amateurs to step over the frontiers of science beside their garden paths.

The work of our Members, our staff and the friendly help of many research stations and Universities through the years, has made the Association what has been described as 'The growing point of the Organic Movement'. Everything that is organic and alive, grows and changes, and from our small beginnings at Bocking, the Association has grown to an organic gardener's equivalent to the Royal Horticultural Society, with the National Centre for Organic Gardening as its 'Wisley'.

Early in the 1980s, the ever-increasing interest in the environment, that began with Rachel Carson's book, *Silent Spring* (Houghton Mifflin, 1962) and our steadily rising membership, convinced us that we had outgrown Bocking, which had parking space only at weekends, too little room for coaches and visitors jammed the narrow paths between experiments on our four Open Days a year. My original vision of a small society of amateur experimenters had grown into a mass movement so we just had to find a new home.

This took two years of searching for somewhere central (instead of near the top left-hand corner of London, so our members and the ever-increasing interested public could converge on it from all sides) and large enough for wide paths, vistas and room to demonstrate as well as experiment, and to grow still larger, for ours is an idea whose time has come.

Our search lead us past a stately home in Dorset, where we might have rented the kitchen gardens, but the National Trust were afraid that we would draw at least 50,000 visitors a year, pulverizing their paths and crowding the car park, because of the interest in organic gardening, and an even statelier home that we could have shared with a huntin', shootin' and fishin' museum in the Shires. Finally, wearied of crumbling greenhouses with rotted rafters and non-standard glass, tree-darkened potting sheds, their steps worn hollow by generations of gardeners and steep twisted lanes with barely room for mini-buses, we found Ryton-on-Dunsmore.

It had been a riding school with 22 acres of land that had not even been limed for thirteen years. It has become the largest chemical-free garden in Britain with eight acres being developed as our organic research station. We sold our beloved Bocking as greedily sought building land and moved to Ryton, with its stables, a giant riding school building, plus a large house for offices. The conversion from riding stables to gardens won us the right to build the bungalow in which I now live on green-belt land that will stay 'green', in both senses, with room for years of growing.

We moved in 1985 and 50,000 visitors came to see the gardens in our first two years. Our membership doubled as we preached to the unconverted by the coachload. We now have over 30 local groups in the UK, three in Australia and one each in India and New Zealand. Our TV series 'All Muck and Magic', other programmes and continued press coverage, maintains our flow of visitors.

The scope of the HDRA has always extended beyond compost heaps, companion planting and pest and disease control without poisons. It encompasses conservation, population and pollution. The work I began in 1976 with desert trees and plants that take in dew through their leaves as Nature's drought defeaters, has grown from my small beginnings to an organic alternative to the dams and pumps that burden the dry Third World with debt and salination. It now includes work with a research station growing 10,000 experimental trees on the almost rainless Cape Verde Islands and co-operation with a Chinese University on a massive experimental enterprise in desert reclamation.

Anyone can join the Association, indeed members range from complete beginner organic gardeners to those who are Professors and have PhDs in Botany. The subscription is £12 a year (£7 for pensioners and the unwaged) and for that members receive a quarterly magazine, an organic gardening advice service and free admission to The National Centre for Organic Gardening, which is worth visiting again and again as it grows and changes through the seasons and because our work expands. It is situated on the B4029, off the A45, five miles south-east of Coventry. If you are interested in learning more about the Association, or have difficulty in obtaining any of the seeds, organic fertilizers, biological pest controls or any other product mentioned in this book, please write to this address for further information, enclosing a stamped addressed envelope.

Henry Doubleday Research Association,
National Centre for Organic Gardening,
Wolston Lane,
Ryton-on-Dunsmore,
Coventry CV8 3LG.

INDEX